SOFTWARE KNOWLEDGE

DEBOJIT ACHARJEE

CONTENTS

Cryptomator: A cloud encryption FOSS

Disk encryption is a technology which converts any data into unreadable code and stores it on a storage device like a hard disk. The unreadable code is decrypted using a key to convert it back to a readable data. This process of encryption/decryption of data on a storage device helps to protect any sensitive data from unauthorized access. There are many types of disk encryption software available online and many are Free Open-Source Software (FOSS) also. Cryptomator (https://cryptomator.org/) is one such disk encryption software that allows to encrypt any data for protection but it is different from any other normal disk encryption software. This software can encrypt any data and let it store on various cloud storage networks like Dropbox and Google Drive. Cryptomator was made by a company called Skymatic GmbH (Germany) in 2016 and was licensed under GPLv3 as a FOSS.

Minimum requirements

The Cryptomator client can run on any desktop PC, laptop or smartphone. For using the latest version of the client software on a desktop PC or laptop – One must have a supported operating system, which includes – Windows 7/8/10, MacOS

10.11/10.12/10.13/10.14/10.15 and TODO Linux. Cryptomator supports Android 4.3/iOS 10.0 or later for using the Cryptomator app on a smartphone. It can be used on a smartphone running supported Android OS/iOS and also compatible with iPad and iPod touch. Cryptomator also requires the latest Java 9 or a newer version to run on any system properly.

Features

Transparent encryption: With this encryption you will not notice any difference in working with your files. Cryptomator creates a virtual hard drive which gets synchronized with the encrypted data on a cloud storage and that data can be easily accessed using the virtual drive. You can work on this drive just like a USB flash drive but the data will be encrypted and stored on any cloud storage like Google drive.

Individual file encryption: Cryptomator can encrypt the files individually and everything you put on the virtual hard drive is encrypted individually in the vault. Compared to other disk encryption utilities, Cryptomator encrypts each file individually, and if you make any change to a file in your vault then that file is only encrypted after being changed. This way the synchronization client of your cloud storage provider knows exactly what needs to be uploaded and what doesn't.

Ease of use and Reliability: The simplicity and ease of use is the key feature of Cryptomator. With Cryptomator you don't have to deal with accounts, key management, cloud access grants or cipher configurations. Just by using a password one can use the vault and can store data on any cloud storage. It's also not required to specify which cloud network to use. It uses transparent data encryption and makes it very easy to store data on any cloud storage. Cryptomator encrypts files and doesn't care where you store them. This makes it a lightweight application and makes it easy to run on any computer or smartphone reliably. Cryptomator also has a feature called Sanitizer, and with this feature it's possible to scan for any corrupted files in the vault. This feature helps troubleshoot any error and makes Cryptomator more reliable in terms of data protection.

Cryptomator

Free client-side encryption for your cloud files.
Open source software: No backdoors, no registration.

Functionality

Cryptomator creates a virtual drive (vault) to add, edit, and remove files as you do with just any disk drive. Files are transparently encrypted using a method called Transparent Data Encryption (TDE). The encrypted data is converted to unreadable code before storing on a cloud storage, and no unencrypted copies are stored on the hard drive. For every encryption a master key is created and stored separately. The encrypted files are decrypted and converted back to readable format using the master key. With every access on your files inside the virtual drive, Cryptomator will encrypt/decrypt these files on-the-fly.

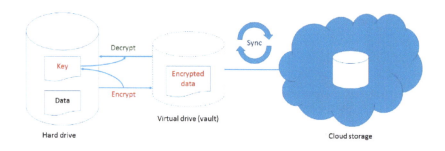

Transparent Data Encryption (TDE)

Currently Dokany (on Windows) and FUSE (on macOS and Linux) are the frontends of choice. If they're not available on your system, Cryptomator will fall back on WebDAV, as it is supported on every major operating system. WebDAV is an HTTP-based protocol and Cryptomator will act as a WebDAV server accepting so-called loopback connections on your computer.

Whenever your file manager accesses files through this virtual drive, Cryptomator will process this request via six layers of encryption and storage methods:

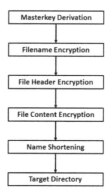

Cryptomator's six layers of encryption and storage methods

1. **Masterkey Derivation:** This is the first layer of encryption and here the masterkey is created for the file that is being stored in the vault. Every vault has its own 256-bit encryption key and both the keys are encrypted using RFC 3394 key wrapping with a KEK derived from the user's password using scrypt. The encrypted keys are stored as integers or Base64 strings in a JSON file named *masterkey.cryptomator*, which is located in the root directory of the vault. When unlocking a vault the KEK is used to unwrap (i.e. decrypt) the stored masterkeys.

2. **Filename Encryption:** In this layer the file and directory names are first encrypted before storing. Initially, each folder gets a unique identifier called directory ID. The directory ID for the root folder is special and always empty. For all other folders a UUID is created. Cryptomator uses AES-SIV to encrypt files as well as directory names and associates according to the ID.

3. **File Header Encryption:** In this layer, the file header stores certain metadata, which is needed for file content encryption. It consists of 88 bytes:

5

- 16 bytes nonce used during header payload encryption.

- 40 bytes AES-CTR encrypted payload that includes 8 bytes filled with 1 for future use (formerly used for file size) and 32 bytes file content key.

- 32 bytes header MAC of the previous 56 bytes.

4. **File Content Encryption:** This layer encrypts the file contents and here the actual file contents get encrypted. The cleartext is broken down into multiple chunks, each up to 32 KB + 48 bytes consisting of:

  - Up to 32 KB encrypted payload using AES-CTR with the file content key.

  - 16 bytes nonce.

  - 32 bytes MAC of file header nonce (to bind this chunk to the file header).

  - Chunk number as 8 byte big endian integer (to prevent undetected reordering).

  - Nonce.

  - Encrypted payload.

  Afterwards, the encrypted chunks are joined preserving the order of the cleartext chunks. The payload of the last chunk may be smaller than 32 KiB.

5. **Name Shortening:** This layer doesn't modify any file contents but it limits the path length to ensure compatibility with certain Microsoft products that do not support long paths. Even with the flattened directory structure achieved during filename encryption, the file

6

path might be longer than 255 characters. If a ciphertext filename exceeds the threshold of 129 characters, it is replaced by its much shorter SHA-1 hash and gets a .lng file extension. Additionally, an equally named metadata file is created in the 'm' directory containing a reverse-mapping back to the original name. This layer doesn't provide any additional security but the main purpose is to maximize compatibility.

6. **Target Directory:** This is the final layer and after the files have been processed by all above layers, they are finally stored into the chosen directory. This is where Cryptomator's final job is done, and lastly the files are synchronized with the cloud storage.

Effectiveness

Cryptomator is a very useful disk encryption FOSS and it can be easily installed on many types of Operating Systems, running on a desktop PC or laptop for free. It can also be used on a smartphone using an Android/iOS app and one can also backup data stored on the smartphone to a cloud storage. However, the cryptomator apps for smartphones are not free to download. Cryptomator uses transparent encryption to store data on a cloud storage and this makes it more secure for storing data on a cloud storage. It also becomes easy and simple for storing data online, because it's compatible with most online cloud storage services like Google drive and Dropbox.

The password used for the Cryptomator vault is not shared online and remains a local password. This makes it more reliable and prevents the chances of online hacking. The encryption used by Cryptomator is also much secured, and it not only encrypts the data but also the encryption keys for security. Cryptomator does the encryption and decryption of data on the fly, that's why Cryptomator is very effective in terms of security and performance. Moreover, as it's an FOSS, it's free from any backdoor or malware issues, and can be trusted for being such a reliable software. It uses Advanced Encryption Standard (AES) method to encrypt the data and the passphrase is protected against brute-force attacks using scrypt – a password-based key derivation function.

Ease of use

Cryptomator is surprisingly very easy to use, and even being a FOSS, it's not like any other FOSS that are difficult to use. It can be easily downloaded from the site https://cryptomator.org/downloads/#winDownload and can be installed on a desktop PC or laptop for free. However Cryptomator has an option for donation on its site and its smartphone apps can be downloaded from the app store by paying online. Cryptomator supports many operating systems like Windows, macOS, Linux, Android and iOS. That's why it's very convenient to run Cryptomator on any computer or smartphone.

The User-Interface (UI) of Cryptomator is also very easy to use both on a computer and a smartphone. The UI is properly designed and its components are well organized – this makes it very easy and convenient to use. Cryptomator also has an online support system for troubleshooting, and anyone can get help online, regarding any problem related to this software. The documentation regarding the use of this software can be found at https://docs.cryptomator.org/en/latest/.

Pros and cons

Pros	Cons
Free to use	No sharing functionality
Open-source and can be modified	No contact options
Easy to use	

Can be used on smartphone also	
Community support available	
Online documentation	

Even though Cryptomator has a few drawbacks, it still beats many other disk encryption FOSS, in terms of functionality and security. Most disk encryption software stores encrypted data locally on a hard drive but Cryptomator makes it possible to store encrypted data on a cloud storage, easily and reliably. Therefore I think with the help of this disk encryption FOSS, we can store our sensitive data on any cloud storage services like Google drive and Dropbox, without any difficulty.

Home automation and security using IoT devices

Home sweet home – that's what everyone thinks about their home but, we can even make our home smarter using technologies like Internet of Things (IoT). IoT is a system in which computing devices are connected over a network using Unique Identifiers (UIDs) and can transfer data without the need of any human-to-human or human-to-computer interaction. Such computing devices are called IoT devices and such devices can be used to automate our home also. The first home automation technology was developed in 1975 that used a network technology called X10. It's a communication protocol used for home automation devices, during that time. It used electric power transmission wiring, for signaling and controlling various electronic devices. The signals used radio frequency as digital data to control any digital electronic device installed in a house. But now technology has changed – with the help of many sophisticated hardware and Free Open-Source Software (FOSS) – home automation can make a dream house come to reality.

Basic setup

The setup for home automation using IoT devices requires a router, connected to the internet and a controller/hub that is connected to the IoT devices/sensors. There are four primary operating standards for home automation technology – Wi-Fi, Z-Wave, Zigbee, and Bluetooth Low Energy (BLE). Wi-Fi is the most commonly used standard for home automation and IoT devices are connected to a centralized controller/hub (either wired or wireless) and it's connected to the router through an Ethernet link. The IoT devices can connect to a cloud network on the internet using the controller/hub and the router. The IoT devices can be controlled through the cloud network using a FOSS or a mobile app.

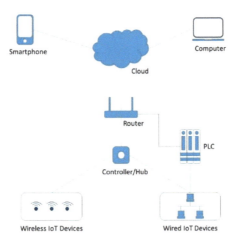

Home automation setup

The mobile app can be used to send and receive data through the cloud network to control and monitor the IoT devices installed in a house. This architecture gives the convenience to control and automate various IoT devices from a distant location with the help of a smartphone and the internet. The IoT devices will be able to send data like room temperature, supply voltage, energy consumption, live video stream, etc. to the smartphone app through the internet and we could monitor our home remotely.

IoT devices/sensors

There are various IoT devices that can be used for home automation and basic IoT devices that are required for the home automation and security are:

- **Wall switches:** IoT based wall switches can be mounted on the wall of a house like any regular wall switches but can be controlled remotely. Such IoT switches can also be wireless and can be connected to an IoT Hub or router wirelessly.

- **Voltage sensors:** IoT voltage sensors can monitor the supply voltage of the house and one can monitor the supply voltage of a house remotely, using the internet.

- **Energy monitors:** IoT Energy monitors are digital energy meters that can monitor the power consumption of the house and one can monitor the overall power consumption remotely with the help of such energy meters.

- **Thermostats:** IoT thermostats can be used to monitor the temperature of the house in real-time. Using such thermostat sensors can help monitor the temperature inside the house from anywhere using the internet.

- **Smart door locks:** Smart door locks are IoT door locks that can be controlled using a home security system and IoT OSS/app over the internet. One can lock and open doors remotely using such IoT door locks using the internet.

- **Air conditioners:** Air conditioning is a very important part of a house and controlling the air conditioner remotely is a part of home automation. IoT based air conditioners can be automated and controlled remotely using an IoT OSS/App connected to the internet.

- **Surveillance cameras:** IoT cameras can be used for the surveillance of the house and they can give the live video footage of the house remotely. Both indoor and outdoor cameras can be used to monitor the indoor and outdoor environments. Such a surveillance system can have features like motion detection and can alert, whenever there is a security breach. Many IoT surveillance OSS/apps can be used to enhance the security and monitoring system of the house.

Apart from the above IoT devices, many other devices can be installed in a house to improve the convenience and automation. Many IoT based home appliances like washing machines, water heaters, refrigerators, dishwashers, robot floor cleaners, etc. can also be installed additionally to improve the automation of the house.

Controller/hub

The controller/hub used for the IoT devices is the main part of the system because it controls all the IoT devices/sensors installed in a house. The connection can be either wired or wireless but wireless is a better option. The controller is connected to the router (gateway) of the house for internet connectivity. The IoT controller/hub uses mainly three types of protocol standards to communicate with the IoT devices – ZigBee, Z-Wave and Wi-Fi. Wink and SmartThings are two most common types of IoT controllers used for home automation. With such a controller/hub it's possible to connect hundreds of IoT devices/sensors in a house and can be controlled with the help of a smartphone app, automatically.

FOSS for home automation

There are various FOSS available for home automation and the most popular ones are:

1. **OpenHAB:** It is a FOSS for home automation written in Java. It is used to connect and control various IoT devices installed in a house. With this app one can perform many operations like switching on lights and fans remotely. One can use various rules to program the automation of the IoT devices, and can also use voice commands to control the devices. The project to develop this app started in 2010 and in 2013, the core functionality became an official project of the Eclipse Foundation under the name Eclipse SmartHome. OpenHAB is not only available for Android OS but also for other systems like Linux, Windows, Mac, Raspberry Pi, PINE A64 and Docker. The app can also connect to the OpenHAB cloud network and the IoT devices of the house can be controlled remotely, using a good internet connection on a smartphone. OpenHAB won the IoT Challenge 2013 and the JavaOne Duke's Choice Award 2013. It was nominated for the JAX Innovation Award 2014 and was the People's Choice Winner at the Postscapes IoT Awards 2014/15.

2. **Jeedom:** This is another FOSS that can be installed on any Linux system and it can also be used on Android/iOS using the smartphone app. It has multiple functionalities like management of scenarios, text/sound interaction with home automation systems, history viewing, and graph generation, linking of all equipment /connected objects and personalization of the interface. The Jeedom mobile application (for iOS / Android) allows you to drive your home automation system and the app automatically connects via a QRcode without the need of any configuration. You will find on your mobile the same functionality to your Jeedom (Scenarios, connected devices and home automation, plugins) and you can also customize your application with shortcuts and more.

   The main features of Jeedom are:

   - Manage the safety of goods and people.

   - Automate heating for better comfort and energy savings.

   - View and manage energy use to anticipate expenses and reduce use.

   - Communicate by voice, SMS, e-mail or mobile applications.

   - Manage all of the home's automatic devices: shutters, gate, lights, etc.

   - Manage multimedia audio and video devices, and connected objects.

   - Jeedon includes its own Market, like what you find on your smartphones with the App Store or Play Store. It allows you to add home automation features and assures the compatibility with new home automation modules, but also lets you customize its fixed and mobile interfaces.

3. **Calaos:** This FOSS lets you control and monitor your home with many features. It can be easily installed and used to transform your home into a smart home. Calaos has a long background in home automation and is built in several different layers. It has Low level as well as uniform and powerful user interfaces. It knows how to talk to hardware, and gives you the convenience to automate your home easily. It was first developed by a French company of the same name but when the company was closed during 2013, the entire code was open sourced and released as GPL. A small community started around the project to continue the development and is growing every day. Calaos can be installed on Linux, Mac, Windows, iOS and Android operating systems. The iOS and Android apps can be used for home automation using a smartphone, remotely. Initially, Calaos supported a special kind of hardware called Programmable Logic Controller (PLC) to automate a building or apartment. PLCs can work as a controller to control various home devices like wall switches, fans, air conditioners, water heaters, etc. but have to be wired to the PLC. However, the newer version of Calaos also supports GPIO, Zibase and IoT devices.

The main features of Calaos are:

- **Hardware support:** Calaos supports hardware like Wago PLC, Raspberry Pi, Zodianet's ZiBASE, Cubieboard, Squeezebox, CCTV, etc. The development community is improving the app to support more hardware arriving in the market. Calaos OS is very easy to install and just by burning a memory card – it's possible to have a complete working software installation.

- **Software stack:** Calaos comes with the following software stack:

  - **Calaos Server:** Core application.

  - **Calaos Home:** Touchscreen user interface.

  - **Calaos Webapp:** HTML5 web application.

  - **Calaos Installer:** Configuration tool.

  - **Calaos iOS:** iOS App.

  - **Calaos Android:** Android App.

  - **Calaos-OS:** Full Linux OS with everything preconfigured.

- **Do It Yourself (DIY):** With Calaos one can quickly and easily install a complete installation. One can get support from the online community regarding any technical issues. The Wiki is full of documentation on how it works, and the Calaos forum can help answer any specific question. One can configure the app as required and as it's an OSS, it's even possible to modify.

Apart from the above three software, there are many more OSS available for home automation but most of them don't support iOS and Android OS for using on a smartphone. Few more OSS that can be used for home automation are Home Assistant, Domoticz, OpenMotics, LinuxMCE, PiDome, MisterHouse and Smarthomatic.

Therefore with the help of proper hardware and software, it's possible to make home automation more secure and smarter. Home automation also saves overall power consumption and helps reduce the electricity bill. As technology improves and more advanced hardware/software comes in the market – home automation will become easier and convenient. Finally someday, a home sweet home will also become a home smart home for everyone.

Artificial Intelligence for pandemic control

Artificial Intelligence (AI) also known as machine intelligence, is a kind of intelligence acquired by computing machines, in order to complete any task that requires human intelligence. With the help of AI the tech industry has improved in almost every sector, and apart from the industrial improvements, AI can also help during any pandemic situation. With the help of various Free Open Source Software (FOSS) tools and using advanced AI hardware – it's possible to develop various AI products that can be used to manage a pandemic. In China, the COVID-19 outbreak was managed using various AI products and services.

Collaborative Development Model

Developing any software including AI, involves designing and coding of various modules, that requires more than one software engineer, especially if it's a large project and needs to be completed in time. In such a case, a collaborative model of software development is useful for developing any software, by distributing its development activity among various people involved in the project. In this model, the development of a software is done in five different stages.

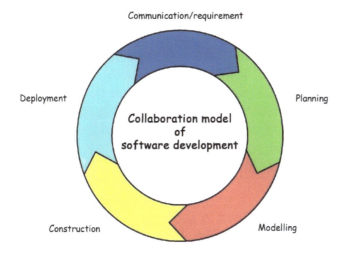

In the beginning, the requirement of a software is gathered from the customer/end-user and the responsibility for communicating with the user is assigned to some people of the project. After gathering the requirement, the planning for the software development is done in the second stage. In this stage software engineers and programmers communicate with each other and do the planning for the software development, which includes creating flowcharts and documentations. In this stage the timeline for the development of the software is also planned. After everything is planned, the software engineers who are assigned for the third stage (modelling) of the project, starts working. In this stage a basic working prototype of the planned software is created. Then comes the fourth stage called construction, and here the actual software is designed and coded. The software testing is also done in this stage by software testers and after successful testing, the software is then taken to the fifth and the final stage – deployment and here the software is released to the customer/end-user. After the user runs the software, the feedback is taken. If any error is found then the software development goes to another iteration of the same development cycle.

In the same way, the collaboration of AI models also helps to develop an effective AI system but here, the collaboration is not only done between the humans, but also with the machines. In this model various machines are connected with each other using a cloud based network and the actual data is stored on the cloud storage and securely exchanged between each other. With this model the connected AI machines can communicate with each other and develop the learning process. Humans can also develop the algorithms stored on cloud storage by following the collaborative model of software development.

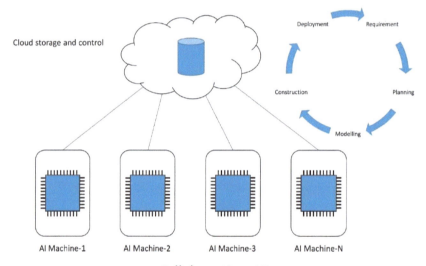

Collaborative AI

In this way the AI machines connected to a cloud network, can improve using the collaborative development model. Collaborative AI works similarly like the collaborative model of software development but the collaboration is done between the machines also.

FOSS tools for AI

There are various Free Open Source Software (FOSS) tools available for the development of AI systems and TensorFlow, Keras, Caffe, OpenNN, Theano, Mycroft and TensorRT are some examples of FOSS tools used for the development of AI systems. Among these tools, TensorFlow and TensorRT are best known for their use in the development of advanced AI systems like autonomous machines.

- **TensorFlow:** It is a FOSS library for dataflow and differentiable programming across a range of tasks. It is a symbolic math library, and is used for machine learning applications such as neural networks. It is used for both research and development of various AI systems. Google used TensorFlow for the development of its various products and was developed by the Google Brain team for internal Google use. It was released under the Apache License 2.0 on November 9, 2015. TensorFlow is available on 64-bit Linux, macOS, Windows, and mobile computing platforms including Android and iOS. In May 2016, Google announced its Tensor Processing Unit (TPU), an application-specific integrated circuit (a hardware chip) built specifically for machine learning and tailored for TensorFlow. It's like an AI accelerator and Google has used TPUs in their data centers also. TensorFlow is an end-to-end open source platform for machine learning and is a rich system for managing all aspects of a machine learning system.

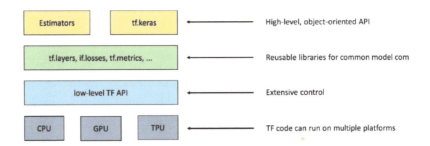

TensorFlow toolkit hierarchy

TensorFlow APIs are arranged hierarchically, and the high-level API is an object-oriented API named tf.keras. It is another API variant of the FOSS tool called Keras and can be used to train machine learning models to make predictions. TensorFlow toolkit also contains reusable libraries that can be used for learning algorithms. The low-level API of TensorFlow is used by many machine learning researchers to create and explore new machine learning algorithms. With the help of the toolkit, it's possible to create the machine learning algorithms that can run on CPU, GPU and TPU also.

- **TensorRT:** It is a free tool from Nvidia that comes as an SDK for the development of high-performance deep learning inference. It includes a deep learning inference optimizer and runtime that delivers low latency and high-throughput for deep learning inference applications. Applications created with TensorRT can perform 40x faster than CPU-only platforms during inference. TensorRT can let you optimize neural network models that are trained in all major frameworks, calibrate them for lower precision with high accuracy and finally, you can deploy them on data centers, embedded systems or any automotive product. TensorRT is also built on Nvidia's

CUDA platform, which is also an API for developing AI systems and it enables you to optimize inference for all deep learning frameworks leveraging libraries, development tools and technologies in CUDA-X for artificial intelligence, autonomous machines, high-performance computing, and graphics. TensorRT provides INT8 and FP16 optimizations for production deployments of deep learning inference applications such as video streaming, speech recognition, recommendation and natural language processing.

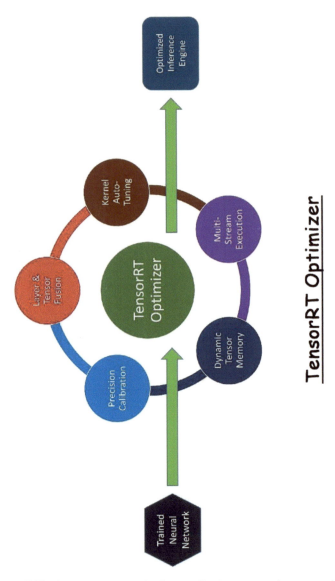

TensorRT has an optimizer that can do precision calibration, layer & tensor fusion, kernel auto-tuning, multi-stream execution and dynamic tensor memory handling. TensorRT optimizes the trained neural network to get an optimized inference engine and makes it possible to train AI machines efficiently.

AI medical assistance apps

Many apps linked with AI systems can be helpful during a pandemic. AI-based Apps that can give medical assistance and keep track of infected individuals, are useful in such situations. There are many cloud-based apps available that can give medical assistance but without AI, such apps won't be able to predict the worst-case scenarios during a pandemic situation. AI-based apps can improve themselves and can find better ways to handle such situations. Such medical assistance apps can give appropriate guidance to the patients according to the level of severity, and some apps with chatbots will even be able to communicate with every individual without the need of any human support. The Software as a service (SaaS) cloud system with AI can be used to give such medical assistance with the help of smartphone apps or any web-based application.

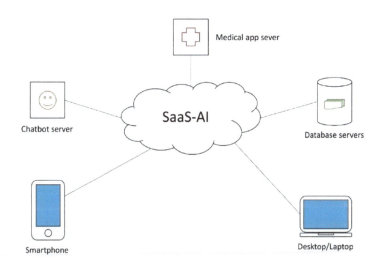

AI cloud medical assistance

During the COVID-19 pandemic in China, apps like Jingdong and Wei Yi, provided online medical consultation services to the patients in China and they work through a cloud-based AI system. Some AI apps like KardiaMobile 6L and TeleICU were also used during the pandemic to monitor patients. A company called AliveCor, launched KardiaMobile 6L, an AI-enabled platform, that allows healthcare professionals to measure QTc (heart rate corrected interval) in COVID-19 patients. The QTc measurement can help detect sudden cardiac arrest and it's based on the FDA's recent guidance to allow more availability of non-invasive remote monitoring devices for the pandemic. Another company called CLEW, launched the TeleICU, and it uses AI to identify respiratory deterioration in advance. Pneumonia is the most common complication of COVID-19 infection, but with the help of AI, now it's possible to detect Pneumonia from analysis of a CT scan in less than sixty seconds with accuracy as high as 92% and a recall rate of 97% on test data sets. This was made possible in China, by an open-source AI model that analyzed CT images and not only identified lesions but also quantified in terms of number, volume and proportion. Therefore, with the help of FOSS tools, it's possible to create such AI medical apps that can help during a pandemic.

Autonomous robots, vehicles and drones

Using service robots can also help people during any pandemic situation. As robots are not affected by any kind of infection, it's possible to deploy many types of service robots to help people who are with any kind of infection. During COVID-19 pandemic, hospitals in China at Guangdong Province used service robots to deliver medicines and communicate with the infected patients. Autonomous vehicles are also useful during any pandemic situation, because such vehicles can drive without the need of any human driver. Such a vehicle uses a variety of sensors like RADAR, LIDAR, Sonar, GPS, odometry and inertial measurement units along with AI algorithms, to drive from one place to another, autonomously. During any pandemic, public transport gets suspended to prevent the spread of infection. In such a crisis, autonomous vehicles can be useful for the transfer and deliver of essential goods. Autonomous drones can also be used to deliver essential goods like food and medicines to the people, during a pandemic. Such a drone uses AI and GPS to self-navigate and can deliver goods to a predefined location. Drones can also be used for the surveillance of huge gathering and monitor restricted places, during a pandemic situation.

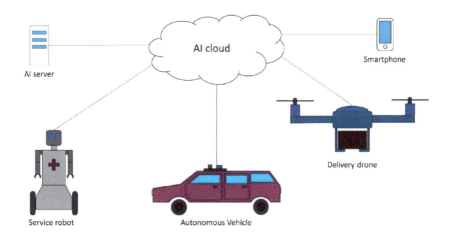

Collaborative AI for autonomous machines

All such autonomous machines like service robots, vehicles and drones can work together using a collaborative development model. Such a collaborative model will make it possible to make such autonomous machines to learn and exchange data efficiently using an AI cloud. With the help of many FOSS tools like TensorRT and hardware like Nvidia AGX, it's possible to create such efficient autonomous machines that can help during a pandemic.

DevOps is the future of software development

DevOps is a method of software engineering which combines both software development (Dev) and Information Technology Operations (Ops) to create high quality software within a short period of time. DevOps shortens the duration of a software development through continuous delivery and integration of code. As the name suggests, DevOps means combination of Development and Operations. Traditionally, software development is done by a team of stakeholders consisting of business analysts, software engineers, programmers and software testers. The software development is done by the development team through a software life cycle consisting of various stages like customer requirement(s), planning, modelling, construction and deployment. However, such a development cycle would take a lot of time and collaboration effort for the successful delivery of the software to the customer. This is also known as agile software development. DevOps can help overcome the drawbacks of agile software development life cycle. In agile method, the software development needs to complete every cycle for it final release and that could take a lot of time for the software to reach maturity but in case of DevOps, instead of delivering the whole software, small chunks of codes are updated and updated software is released to the operations team in a continuous manner, which improves the software development cycle. DevOps lifecycle can be automated using various development tools and requires less manual activity. The idea first came in 2008 with a discussion between Patrick Debois and Andrew Clay Shafer concerning the DevOps concept. However, the idea only started to spread in 2009 with the advent of the first DevOpsDays event held in Belgium. Now, most of the tech giants like Facebooks, Google, Amazon, Netflix, etc., have adopted the DevOps culture.

DevOps LifeCycle and Tools

DevOps lifecycle consists of eight stages – plan, code, build, test, release, deploy, operate and monitor. There are also various Free Open Source Software (FOSS) tools that can be used to improve and automate the DevOps life cycle.

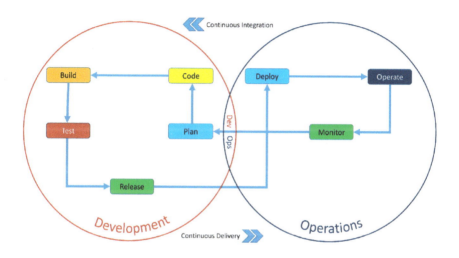

DevOps Life Cycle

Eight stages of DevOps are explained below:

- **Plan:** This is the starting stage of DevOps where the planning for the software development is done by the development team. Everything from the software requirements to development timeline are planned and the development team works accordingly. FOSS tools like Redmine, Trac and Git are used in this stage.

- **Code:** After everything is planned, the coding for the software development is done at this stage. Coding can be done from scratch or can be reused according to the requirements. Many FOSS tools can be used for coding

31

and Git is one such tool that is used to automate the process.

- **Build:** After the coding is done, it is shared with other software engineers of the development team. After reviewing the code, it is either approved or rejected but if it's approved, then it is merged with the main codebase of the repository. FOSS tools like Gradle can be used to automate this process.

- **Test:** Once the new code is merged with the codebase, it is tested on a virtual environment, using a VM or Kubernetes. At this stage the new code is tested using a series of both manual and automated tests. This is the most crucial stage of DevOps and should go through without failure. This stage could also cause bottlenecks and increase the timeline. In order to complete the stage successfully without much delay, various continuous testing tools are used. FOSS tools like CruiseControl and Selenium are used to automate the process.

- **Release:** After the code is tested successfully, it is prepared for release. At this stage the development team decides which features of the software product should be enabled or disabled by default, and when it should be released. This is the final stage for the development cycle of DevOps and after this the delivery of the software/code is done to the operations team. This stage can also be automated using FOOS tools like Jenkins and Bamboo.

- **Deploy:** This stage belongs to the operations team and it starts after the release of the software by the development team. The software is then deployed by the operations team using various tools. At this stage, it's configured according to the requirements of the operations team. FOSS tools like Puppet, Ansible and Saltstack are used to automate the deployment process.

- **Operate:** After the software has been updated and configured, the operations team starts operating their products and services with the updated software. This is done either using their proprietary or FOSS tools.

- **Monitor:** This is the final stage for the IT operations team and also for the DevOps life cycle. Here the customer requirements are gathered and the data is sent to the development team to update the software product/service for the next iteration of DevOps. A FOSS tool like Nagios is used by the operations team to automate the monitoring process.

Benefits of DevOps

DevOps have many benefits over the agile software development process. In the case of an agile software development lifecycle, the development process can progress through four main stages – planning, coding, testing and release. The planning for the software development is done based on the customer requirements and it involves assigning various tasks to the stakeholders, like designing flowcharts, writing documentation, estimating timeline, etc. After planning is done, the coding for the software development starts and a working prototype is created. The prototype is then tested in the 3rd stage (testing stage). Testing stage is the most important part of the agile software development life cycle because this stage can affect the overall quality of the software. This stage can also cause bottlenecks because the time required for software testing cannot be estimated precisely and could go beyond the project's timeline. After successfully testing the software, it is then released to the customer in the 4th stage. However, if the customer finds any problem with the software then the development team takes the customer's feedback for another iteration of the development cycle. Then the whole development process takes place again with the four stages to improve the software and then it is released again, with another version number. Then again the customer's feedback is taken and if any improvement is required then the development cycle goes into iteration again and the cycle keeps on continuing until the software reaches maturity (stable software). This type of development cycle could take an indefinite amount of time and causes delay in software development. That's why using DevOps can make the development cycle quicker and effective. As in DevOps the communication of the development team is done with the operations team instead of the customer, the development team doesn't have to take the burden of the customers. In DevOps only small chunks of codes are continuously coded and tested, which prevents any bottleneck or delay in delivery of the code. DevOps provides continuous delivery and integration of the code. This is why DevOps is better than the agile software development methodology.

As DevOps has many benefits over agile software development methodology, many software companies are resorting to DevOps culture. As DevOps provides continuous delivery and integration, it can help software products and services to reach maturity in a very short period of time. DevOps is mainly suitable for the development of cloud computing products and services, because it needs a collaboration between the development team and the IT operations. As there is a growing demand for cloud computing products and services, DevOps will be the right choice for most software companies. Therefore, DevOps can help improve the software development process efficiently and has a great future ahead.

Importance of blockchain for COVID-19

Blockchain is a technology that can store any data securely using a chain of blocks that are linked using cryptography. As the name suggests – it's a chain of blocks that carry data (usually about any transaction) and hashes (created for the linked blocks). It is a unique method of storing data in a distributed manner and that also makes it a very secure data storage system. This way of storing data using a chain of blocks linked together with cryptography, was first described by Stuart Haber and W. Scott Stornetta. However, this technology was improved by Satoshi Nakamoto in 2008 and implemented with a cryptocurrency called Bitcoin. Apart from Bitcoin, many financial services, logistic companies and social media giants are now trying to implement blockchain for their products and services.

Blockchain architecture

A blockchain consists of blocks (a virtual data container) that contain data and a hash. The hash is created based on the data stored in the block and it is done with the help of a hash creation algorithm. The block also contains the hash of its previous block. A block is created whenever any new data is stored in the blockchain network or any transaction is done (in case of cryptocurrency).

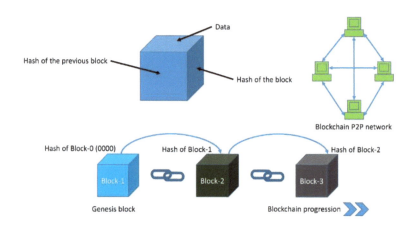

Blockchain Architecture

Blockchain uses a Peer-to-peer (P2P) network and whenever a new block is created, it is linked with the previous block in the network by storing the hash of the previous block in it. This makes a block chain secure because if the data of any block is tampered then it will change the hash of that block and it will no longer be connected with the blockchain. Blockchain also uses a timestamp for every data stored in a block and that prevents it from tampering or copying. While timestamping, the exact time of the stored data is stamped (stored) inside the block along with the data. If any change is made to the data then the time also changes. This feature of blockchain makes it sure for cryptocurrencies, because if any transaction data is tampered then the time of transaction also changes. Almost any kind of data can be stored in a block chain but in case of crypto currencies, data related to the user and transaction data are mainly stored, which is also known as distributed ledger. Crypto currencies like Bitcoin use a concept called proof of work, which is carried out usually by the bitcoin miners, in order to validate any transaction over the blockchain network. Bitcoin miners are users who use powerful computing machines (ASIC processors) to solve certain mathematical problems in a network. Such machines are like super computers, specially designed for processing data over a bitcoin network. The efficiency of a mining machine is measured in terahash and today at least 12 terahash/sec speed is required for mining Bitcoins. More powerful the miner is, the more there is a chance of solving the math problems and the miner who solves it first, gets the chance to create the next block and validates any transaction on the bitcoin network. However, the Proof of Work (PoW) concept requires a lot of electricity and computing power because such ASIC machines need a lot of electrical power to operate. However, some cryptocurrencies uses Proof of Stake (PoS), where the creator for the next block is randomly chosen based on the wealth and age (i.e., the stake) but such cryptocurrencies are more vulnerable to fake stake attacks, because the attacker can cash an affected node by using very little or no stake.

A blockchain operates mainly through four layers – User Interface (UI) layer, application layer, consensus/validation layer and data layer.

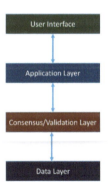

Blockchain Layers

The User Interface (UI) layer is the top most layer and it helps the user interact with the blockchain network. Application layer is the 2nd layer and any app that uses a blockchain operates in this layer. Then comes the consensus/validation layer, where, the instructions sent by the apps are validated in this layer by the algorithms of the blockchain network and in case of cryptocurrencies, Proof of Work (PoW) and Proof of Stake (PoS) works in this layer. Finally comes the data layer and here the processing of the data is done, like storing and retrieving of data from the blocks.

Use of block chain for COVID-19

Blockchain can be very useful in many ways during any pandemic like COVID-19 and can be used for cryptocurrency, Supply Chain Management (SCM) and infection tracking. As blockchain seems more reliable and secured, using a blockchain network for COVID-19 can help people manage their life and also control the pandemic.

- **Cryptocurrency:** Using cryptocurrencies based on blockchain during and after COVID-19 can help people to make any financial transaction, reliably and flawlessly. As coronavirus can also transmit through currency notes and social distancing is the primary preventive measure for COVID-19, using cryptocurrencies like Bitcoin can help control the pandemic. When compared with other digital payments like debit/credit cards, Electronic Funds Transfer (EFT)/Wire transfer and online wallets, cryptocurrencies on blockchain networks are more reliable and less prone to hacking. Moreover, any kind of centralized online payment services could go down because of any technical problem or virus attacks, but as blockchain is always a decentralized network, cryptocurrencies like bitcoin are less vulnerable to such problems. Maybe because of such benefits, the Supreme Court has lifted the ban on Bitcoin in India, which was imposed by BRI in 2018. The value of one Bitcoin remained above $5000 (Rs 4,00,000) for the last one year and reached its highest value ($12,927.40) on 26-June-2019. One can buy and trade bitcoins in India through various trading companies like BuyUcoin and

Zebpay. Bitcoin uses Secure Hash Algorithm (SHA) for its blockchain network and as the name suggests, it's a secure algorithm that prevents any kind of hacking attacks. Apart from Bitcoins, one can also trade other cryptocurrencies like Bitcoin Cash, Ethereum and Litecoin on such platforms. However, all types of cryptocurrencies don't use Proof of Work (PoW) and currencies like Peercoin, Nxt and PotCoin use either Proof of Stake (PoS) or both. As Proof of Stake (PoS) is not so reliable than Proof of Work (PoW), Bitcoin is much more reliable when compared with other cryptocurrencies that use only Proof of Stake (PoS). Facebook is planning to launch their digital currency called Libra that will use blockchain for any transaction and is based on an open source model.

- **Supply Chain Management (SCM):** Delivery of essential items like food and medicines are important during any pandemic and it's the SCM that makes it possible for such delivery. SCM is the process of keeping track of goods and inventories in a way that would help the logistics team to deliver items on time. With the help of a good SCM system one can get the transit information of a shipment and can track it from point to point. Artificial Intelligence (AI) can also help to control the SCM to get better results and would require less human effort. However, any SCM requires storage of data into a data storage system like a centralized server or a cloud storage, but such a storage system could be vulnerable to virus or hacking attacks. Even any fraudulent interception of any shipment can happen on any centralized SCM system. As blockchain is always decentralized, no such fraudulent activity can happen easily on any SCM that uses a blockchain network. During a pandemic like COVID-19, the need for essential goods is highly expected by people around the globe, and such a high demand for goods can only be fulfilled by reliable logistics, with the help of a SCM system that uses blockchain. Many logistics companies like Maersk,

FedEx, DHL and UPS are using blockchain for their operations.

- **Infection tracking:** During a pandemic, tracking of individuals with active infection is very important and this is done with the help of various screening processes. For COVID-19, the screening of infection is done at various entry points like airports and railway stations. This screening is done using thermal scanners, and if any person had fever then the thermal scanner would detect it. Then the suspected person would be sent for quarantine. Such quarantined people are digitally marked through their smartphones. That's why some mobile apps can help to identify people who are already quarantined or marked by the medical authorities for having COVID-19 infection. Apps like Aarogya Setu, can help people to keep social distance and this app can detect any infected person within close range. Such an app uses Bluetooth and GPS to detect any infected person who is also using the same app. Some apps can even tell which hospitals are available for COVID-19 patients and how many beds are available. However, such apps are using a centralized or a cloud based network but are not always reliable. Using a blockchain network for storing data about the COVID-19 patients would make it safe and reliable. As every block in a blockchain is tamper proof, the data stored on such a network will always be safe and secured. As blockchain networks are less vulnerable to fraudulent attacks, the infection tracking information stored on such networks will not be affected in any manner. Moreover, most infection tracking systems used by the government are centralized and cannot be used outside the country. Such a centralized tracking system has limitations, and if any infected person moves outside the country then it will not be detected by other countries. As blockchain is a decentralized system, it can be used by any user around the globe and the information about an infected individual will be shared with every user of the blockchain. This will be able to alert a COVID-19 infected person even if that person travels to another country. Therefore, using blockchain for infection tracking can be very useful in pandemics like COVID-19.

Pros and cons

Pros	Cons
• **Decentralized:** The decentralized network of blockchain gives the users to control it, instead of any centralized network. This prevents any unfair activity over a network and gives equal rights to all its users. • **Transparency:** Blockchain is a transparent network and all stored data is shared with every user or node in the network. This makes the data transparent to every user and prevents any unknown data tamper. It is especially useful for cryptocurrencies and if any fraudulent transaction is done by an attacker, then everyone in the network would know about it. • **Anonymity:** Blockchain uses a network where every	• **Performance:** The decentralized nature of blockchain makes it a slow and time consuming network. When compared to other cloud based networks, the speed and performance of any blockchain network can vary depending on the users and the computers used by the users. In case of cryptocurrencies like Bitcoin, the speed of the miners can affect the performance of the network. • **Power consumption:** The power consumption of the ASIC machines used for mining can vary depending on the processing power. Higher the processing power of the machine, more the power it will consume.

41

user remains anonymous and this gives full privacy to the users. Such anonymity also protects the users from any kind of identity theft. Hence, any type of users including big organizations can also use a cryptocurrency of a blockchain to do any kind of transaction. • **Security:** As blockchain uses a decentralized network and every user is anonymous, it is difficult for hackers or computer viruses to attack the network easily. Moreover, cryptocurrencies that use Proof of Work (PoW) for the blockchain are more secured and transactions are often reliable.	

Blockchain is a unique way of storing data over a network, and because of its exceptional features, it's been accepted by many companies for their products and services. Even though blockchain has a few drawbacks, its benefits and advantages outweighs its disadvantages. Therefore, blockchain can be very useful during a pandemic like COVID-19.

MyRocks DB engine of Facebook truly rocks!

As data is the basic requirement of any software system, storing data adequately is the biggest challenge. That's where a database comes into use, and a database can organise, store and retrieve data from a computer storage system using a software. Such a software is known as Database Management System (DBMS) and it helps the users and applications to store or retrieve data from a database. However, when the database is too large and on a cloud network or server, then it becomes tedious to store and retrieve data effectively. That's why a database engine is needed with a DBMS to perform database operations with minimum latency. Various DBMS like MySQL, PostgreSQL, MSSQL, Oracle Database, and Microsoft Access can be used with a database server. Such types of DBMS software were being used with a database server that uses a traditional magnetic hard drive. However, magnetic drives could cause a lot of latency when compared to a *Solid State Drive (SSD)*. As SSDs use flash memory chips instead of any magnetic disk or any mechanical moving parts, the read/write speed of SSDs is faster than any traditional magnetic drive. That's why such SSDs can be used in a database server to store/retrieve data with minimum latency. However, to make use of SSD technology with a database server, a special database software is required. That's where RocksDB comes into use, and with the help of RocksDB, it's possible to use

SSDs in a database server. It's an embedded database that can be used with SSDs and requires very less maintenance. This was created by Facebook in May 2012, using C++ programming language, in order to overcome the disadvantages of InnoDB, which caused read/write/space amplification factors. However, Facebook wanted to use MySQL features with the database servers that are using SSDs. As MySQL is great for backup and automation, Facebook wanted to make use of this DBMS along with RocksDB. That's why Facebook developed the MyRocks database engine in 2015 and it was also written in C++. MyRocks integrates the RocksDB and MySQL in such a way that SQL can be used by the Facebook applications with the RocksDB database server. MyRocks is an open source database engine that helps to store/retrieve data from an embedded database like RocksDB using MySQL.

Requirements and limitations

- MyRocks requires C++ compilers and libraries for development.

- MyRocks works with RocksDB to implement the MySQL layer.

- It is based on Oracle MySQL 5.6.

- MyRocks is included from MariaDB 10.2.5.

- MyRocks requires MariaDB server on Linux and Windows.

- MyRocks builds are available on platforms that support a sufficiently modern compilers like Ubuntu Trusty, Xenial, (amd64 and ppc64el), Ubuntu Yakkety (amd64), Debian Jessie, stable (amd64, ppc64el), Debian Stretch, Sid (testing and unstable) (amd64).

- CentOS/RHEL 7 (amd64), Centos/RHEL 7.3 (amd64), Fedora 24 and 25 (amd64), OpenSUSE 42 (amd64) and Windows 64 (zip and MSI).

- Maria DB optimistic parallel replication may not be supported.

- MyRocks is not available for 32-bit platforms.

- Galera Cluster is tightly integrated into InnoDB storage engine (it also supports Percona's XtraDB which is a modified version of InnoDB). Galera Cluster does not work with any other storage engines, including MyRocks (or TokuDB for example).

Functionality and architecture

MyRocks is a database engine and any database engine is used by the DBMS to *create, read, update and delete (CRUD)* data from a database. Information in a database is stored as bits laid out as data structures in a storage that can be efficiently read from and written to the properties of a hardware. There are various types of data structures – Linear, Trees, Hash-based and Graphs. Most database engines use trees (data structure) for storing and retrieving data. The most commonly used data structure for trees is the B tree, and database engines use this type of data structure for storing/retrieving data. Some even use the *Indexed Sequential Access Method (ISAM)* but B tree is more popular.

In a B tree storage system, keys and data are stored as nodes and it starts with a root node and it is connected to other parent and child nodes. This process of data storage makes it easier for data insertion and deletion. However, B+ tree is a newer extension of the B tree, and it is more efficient for data insertion, deletion and search operations. It consists of a root, internal nodes and leaves, the root may be either a leaf or a node with two or more children. In B tree, both the data and keys are stored in the internal and leaf nodes but B+ tree can store data only in the leaf nodes, and stores the keys in the internal nodes. The leaf nodes of a B+ tree are linked together like a single linked list and this makes the search operation more efficient.

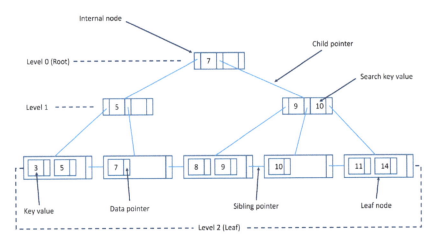

B+ tree data structure

B+ tree are used to store a large amount of data which cannot be stored in the main memory. As size of the main memory is often limited, the internal nodes (keys to access records) of the B+ tree are stored in the main memory whereas leaf nodes (containing data) are stored in the secondary memory. The internal nodes of B+ tree are also called index nodes because they always point to the leaf nodes that contain the actual data. A B+ tree (except the root node), can have M/2 minimum internal and leaf nodes (where 'M' is the maximum number of nodes except the root node) and can have M − 1 leaf nodes.

B+ tree search algorithms are used to search data efficiently and can be as follows:

1. Call the binary search method on the nodes of the B+ tree.
2. If the search parameters are matched then:
   The accurate result is returned and displayed to the user.
   Else, if the node being searched is the current and the exact key is not found:
   Display the statement "Recordset cannot be found!".

However, such B+ tree algorithm may be efficient but still the database can have poor performance during random access. That's why using RocksDB can resolve this problem because it uses a data structure called *Log Structured Merge Tree (LSMT)*. LSMT uses a hybrid kind of data structure and combines various components of data structures to store/retrieve data. It is seen that sequential access is faster than random access, whether it's a magnetic storage or an SSD. As B+ tree allows both random and sequential access, during the random access operations, the performance of the database can be affected, even when used with SSDs. That's why LSMT is used by RocksDB to overcome this problem.

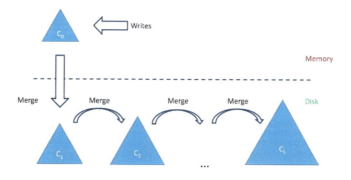

Log Structured Merge Tree (LSMT) data structure

In LSMT, data is structured as logs in various levels and stored in the memory and disk. A minimum two-level LSMT uses two logs, one for the memory and another for the disk storage (flash/SSD). For example, C_0 is the top level log and stays in the memory. Whereas, C_1 is a segment of C_0 but stored in the disk and elements are inserted in the C_0 log. When the size of the log exceeds the memory, the log is merged with the C_1 log on the disk. Similarly, more than two levels can have more merges and logs, like C_2, C_3, C_4... C_L logs (L = total number of levels). As the latency of the main memory is less than the disk, storing recently updated logs in the memory can improve the performance of the database. This method of storing data is relevant to sequential access and has better IO throughput.

Using RocksDB with LSMT improves the performance of the embedded database but using a good DBMS also helps automate and maintain the database efficiently. MySQL is one such DBSM that can perform various types of database operations using the *Structured Query Language (SQL)*. SQL is a language that programmers use to create, modify and extract data from the relational database and also control user access to the database. It is an open-source *Relational Database Management System (RDBMS)*, which organizes data into one or more data tables in which data types may be related to each other and these relations help structure the data.

SQL language uses *Keywords, Identifiers, Clauses, Expressions, Predicates, Queries, Statements* and *Insignificant whitespace*. *Keywords* are words that are defined in the SQL language. They are either reserved (e.g. SELECT, COUNT and YEAR), or non-reserved (e.g. ASC, DOMAIN and KEY). *Identifiers* are names on database objects, like tables, columns and schemas. An identifier may not be equal to a reserved keyword, unless it is a delimited identifier (identifiers enclosed in double quotation marks) and can contain characters normally not supported in SQL identifiers, and they can also be identical to a reserved word, e.g. "COUNT". *Clauses* are constituent components of statements and queries. *Expressions* can update values or change columns and rows of data in a table. *Predicates* are used for conditional statements to evaluate three-value logic (true/false/unknown) or Boolean truth values. *Queries* help retrieve the data based on specific criteria and it's an important element of SQL. *Statements* are used to do many database operations like transactions, database automation and diagnostics. *Insignificant whitespace* is generally ignored in SQL statements and queries, making it easier to format SQL code for readability.

SQL can be used to perform various logical operations on database, for example:

```
CASE n WHEN 0
        THEN 'Zero'
    WHEN 1
        THEN 'One'
    ELSE 'Out of range!'
END
```

The above SQL 'CASE' statement is useful for conditional database operations.

Queries are important operations of SQL for any database, for example:

```
SELECT Car.brand AS Brand,
    count(*) AS Company
 FROM  Car
 JOIN  Car_company
  ON  Car.price = Car_company.price
 GROUP BY Brand;
```

The above statement uses the 'SELECT' clause to retrieve data about the cars from an inventory database of sellers based on price and brand.

As SQL operations are important for database operations, MyRocks is used with RocksDB to support MySQL. MyRocks integrates RocksDB with MySQL and helps to run SQL commands. MyRocks is a database engine that stores data using the RocksDB as *Static Sorted Table (SST)* files in the SSDs. Such files are segmented using the *Log Structured Merge Tree (LSMT)* concept and stored in the disk.

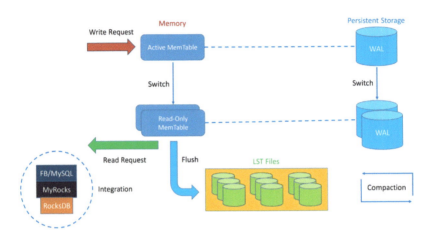

MyRocks/RocksDB Architecture

Any write request made to the memory is stored in the *Active Memtable* and another copy is created as *Read-Only Memtable (ROM)*. When the data exceeds the memory, it is flushed to the disk as SST files using the LSMT concept. Simultaneously, log files called *Write Ahead Log (WAL)* are created and stored separately on the disk. These log files are later used to restore any data after any system failure. During any read request, the ROM is used from the memory to retrieve any data. MyRocks integrates RocksDB and MySQL to perform these operations flawlessly, using SQL.

Features

MyRocks makes it possible to run MySQL with RocksDB and has the following features:

s

- **Greater Space Efficiency:** MyRocks has 2x better compression compared to compressed InnoDB and 3-4x better compression compared to uncompressed InnoDB. This makes it possible to use less space.

- **Greater Writing Efficiency:** MyRocks has a 10x less write amplification compared to InnoDB and gives better endurance of flash storage, which improves the overall throughput.

- **Faster Replication:** No random reads for updating secondary keys, except for unique indexes. The Read-Free Replication option restricts any random reads when updating primary keys and this makes faster replication.

- **Faster Data Loading:** MyRocks writes data directly onto the bottommost level and avoids all compaction overheads when you enable faster data loading for a session.

Pros and cons

Pros	Cons
• MyRocks integrates RocksDB with MySQL and makes it possible to use SQL for the embedded database.	• MyRocks doesn't make use of additional memory like InnoDB and it doesn't benefit from increasing the memory size.
• MyRocks was 2x smaller than InnoDB (compressed) and 3.5x smaller than InnoDB (uncompressed).	• The read amplification of MyRocks can be improved with additional memory but still remains greater than InnoDB.
• MyRocks does not require a lot of memory and performs the IO operations	• MyRocks uses a lot of CPU no matter how much memory is allocated to it and

constantly, while using most of the CPU resources. • MyRocks is a write-optimized engine and reduces the write amplification up to a greater extent.	that's why its performance is limited to the CPU.

MyRocks is a unique database engine designed by Facebook to work with RocksDB so that MySQL can be used with the database. Even though InnoDB seems better than MyRocks in certain ways, it cannot give such functionality to use MySQL with an embedded database. Therefore, MyRocks is better than InnoDB and it truly rocks!

Google Fuchsia is better than Android OS

If hardware is the heart of a computer, then the Operating System (OS) is its soul and without an OS, the computer is just a piece of dead hardware. It's the OS that gives life to a computer and makes it perform various tasks. That's why it's important to choose the right OS for a particular computer system. The design and development of an OS plays an important role for the computer hardware and a perfectly designed OS can make the hardware running at its full potential. Basically, there are 7 types of OS – *Single-tasking and multitasking*, *Single and multi-user*, *Distributed*, *Templated*, *Embedded*, *Real-time* and *Library*. Among these, the Single-tasking and multitasking OS is more widely used in many computer systems. Multi-tasking OS, which is also generally known as General Purpose OS (GPOS), is mostly used because of its ability to do multiple tasks at the same time and GPOS like Mac, Windows, Linux, Android and Raspberry Pi are currently used because of their multi-tasking ability. Such GPOS works by a method called time-slicing and here, the OS slices the CPU time into various time slots. Each time slot is dedicated to a task and they are scheduled accordingly, this process is also known as preemptive multitasking. The time scheduling of the task is done in such a way that the system throughput is maintained but GPOS don't give time assurance

53

for completion of any task because tasks are not executed based on their priority basis and can cause latency. Whereas, in case of a Real Time OS (RTOS), every task is executed according to the priority and can complete a task within the expected time. That's why RTOS doesn't cause any latency like the GPOS and is more responsive to the I/O data. As most of the smartphones use Android and iOS, the user experiences some kind of latency at some point of time because both the OS uses preemptive multitasking and are not RTOS. Moreover, Google developed Android OS from the kernel of Linux OS, which was not designed for the smartphone hardware and to compensate this incompatibility, Android OS uses middleware to support the hardware. Whereas, Apple developed the iOS by shrinking the Mac OS, and as the hardware for iPhone was designed for iOS, there were no compatibility issues like Android. Android OS also suffers from fragmentation at some point of time. Because of this reason, Android smartphones get performance issues after some use. RTOS can not only improve the performance of smartphones but also IoT devices and as the I/O response of RTOS is better than GPOS, IoT devices can be controlled with minimum latency.

Therefore, to get a better solution, Google is now working on the development of a new OS called Fuchsia. Google Fuchsia is an open source RTOS that is capable of running on many platforms, from embedded systems to smartphones, tablets, and personal computers. As Fuchsia is RTOS, it will not cause any latency and performance issues like the Android OS. In contrast to prior Google-developed operating systems such as Chrome OS and Android, which are based on the Linux kernel, Fuchsia is based on a new kernel called Zircon, named after the mineral. Zircon is derived from Little Kernel, a small operating system intended for embedded systems. "Little Kernel" was developed by Travis Geiselbrecht, a creator of the NewOS kernel used by Haiku. The initial development of Fuchsia started at GitHub. On July 1, 2019, Google announced the official website (https://fuchsia.dev) of the development project providing source code and documentation for the operating system.

Requirements

- Google Fuchsia can be improved and customized using various programming languages and runtimes, including C++, Rust, Flutter, and Web.

- Flutter - a software development kit is required to code the apps and UI for Fuchsia.

- A 64-bit Intel machine with at least 8GB of RAM and 100GB of free disk space is required to develop Fuchsia.

- One of the best ways to experience Fuchsia is by running it on actual hardware like Acer Switch 12, Intel NUC, and Google Pixelbook.

- The Fuchsia install process, called 'paving', requires two connected machines over a network, the machine on which you want to run Fuchsia ("target") and the machine on which you build Fuchsia ("host").

- Fuchsia creates a Unix-like file system called MinFS and can currently support files up to 4G.

- Fuchsia requires AArch64 (ARM64) and x86-64 platforms to run.

Functionality/Architecture

Google Fuchsia doesn't use a microkernel but uses a different type of kernel called message passing. A message passing kernel is one kind of Inter Process Communication (IPC) mechanism, where processes communicate with each other by passing messages. Unlike the shared memory kernel, which is also another kind of IPC, a message passing kernel doesn't share the memory with the processes but uses a message queue instead.

In a message passing kernel, one process can send a message to another through the message queue and the message carries the information about the requirement. Each message that is sent by a process, contains the identity of the process that is going to receive it. Similarly, the process that receives the message, creates another message and sends it back to the previous process and informs about the requirement. In this way messages are passed between every process of the kernel without any flaw.

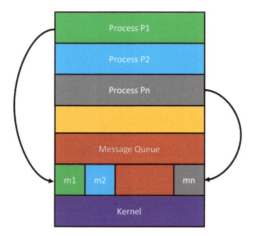

Message passing process

If there are two processes (P1 and P2) running by the kernel and P1 needs to use a resource that is being currently used by the process P2, then P1 will send a message to P2 to release the resource within a specified time. As soon as P2 will receive the message, it will try to complete its process within the time specified by P1 and the kernel will give higher priority to P2. After completing the process, P2 will then inform P1 by passing a message that the resource is free to use and P1 will use the resource after getting the message. This process of message passing can keep the system running without any latency, and is also easier to implement than a shared memory process.

Fuchsia has four layers and are as follows:

- **Zircon:** This is the 1st layer and is a kernel of Fuchsia. Zircon is composed of a new kind of message passing kernel derived from Linux, called the little kernel. This is the heart of Fuchsia and was designed by Google to work with all kinds of devices like smartphones, laptops and IoT devices. This layer mediates hardware access, implements essential software abstractions over shared resources, and provides a platform for low-level software development.

- **Garnet:** It is the 2nd layer that provides device-level system services for software installation, administration, communication with remote systems, and product deployment. This layer contains the network, media, and graphics services and also contains the package management and update system.

- **Peridot:** This 3rd layer provides the services needed to create a cohesive, customizable, multi-device user experience assembled from modules, stories, agents, entities, and other components. It contains the device, user, story runners and also the ledger and resolver, as well as the context and suggestion engines.

- **Topaz:** It is the top most 4th layer that increases system functionality by implementing interfaces defined by underlying layers and it contains four major categories of software: modules, agents, shells, and runners. Modules include the calendar, email, and terminal modules, shells include the base shell and the user shell, agents include the email and chat content providers, and runners include the Web, Dart, and Flutter runners.

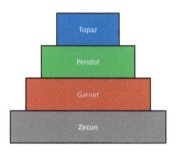

Fuchsia Layers

Google Fuchsia is coded using C, C++, Dart, Go, Rust and Python language. It can support machines with ARM64 and x86-64 architectures. The Flutter development kit produces apps based on Dart, offering apps with high performance that can run at 120 frames per second. Fuchsia also offers a Vulkan-based graphics rendering engine called Escher, with specific support for "Volumetric soft shadows". A special version of Android Runtime for Fuchsia will be developed and it will run on machines with this system from a FAR file, the equivalent of the Android APK.

Security
Google Fuchsia uses a concept called Sandboxing, which prevents the apps from gaining full access to the OS. All access to the kernel of the OS is exposed to the apps as object-capabilities, which means that applications running on Fuchsia have no ambient authority: applications can interact only with the objects to which they have been granted access explicitly. Software is delivered in hermetic packages and everything is sandboxed, which means all software that runs on the system, including applications and system components, receives the least privilege to perform any operation and gains access only

to the information it needs to know. Such an architecture will keep the kernel safe and can prevent any venerable attacks.

Features

- Fuchsia's user interface and apps are written with a software development kit called Flutter and it allows cross-platform development abilities for Fuchsia, Android and iOS.

- Due to the cross-platform opportunities offered by the Flutter development kit, users are able to install parts of Fuchsia on Android devices also.

- Fuchsia is designed to be updatable and packages are designed to be updated independently or even delivered ephemerally and the software is always up-to-date, like a Web page.

- Fuchsia currently supports many types of languages and runtimes, including C++, Rust, Flutter, and Web. Developers can use a variety of languages or runtimes without needing to change Fuchsia itself.

- Fuchsia is designed for optimised performance and use of asynchronous message passing communication reduces latency by letting the sender proceed without waiting for the receiver. It also optimizes memory use by avoiding garbage collection in the core operating system, which helps to minimize memory requirements to achieve equivalent performance.

Pros and cons

Pros	Cons
• Fuchsia supports many languages like C, C++, Dart,	• Fuchsia uses a message passing kernel instead of a shared memory,

Go, Rust and Python.

- Fuchsia can be developed using a development kit called Flutter, which can also be used to create cross-platform apps for Fuchsia, Android and iOS.

- Fuchsia can also support Android apps (APK) by using a runtime.

- Fuchsia can support both ARM-46 and x86-64 architecture and can run on Laptops, smartphones and IoT devices.

- Fuchsia uses a sandboxing concept to run the apps and this makes it a much secured OS by preventing any attacks.

the system has slower communication and the connection time between the processes may take some time.

- Fuchsia will be using a UI which is different from Android and current Android users might find it difficult to use.

Google Fuchsia is a new open-source RTOS that will come with various improved features compared to Android and can help various IoT devices to work effectively. This operating system was chosen by Google to overcome the drawbacks of the Android OS, and that's why it will give a better user experience.

Cloud Foundry is the best open-source PaaS

CLOUD**FOUNDRY**

Platform as a service (PaaS) is a kind of cloud computing service that provides a platform to the developers and software engineers to develop, run, and manage applications without the need of building and maintaining the infrastructure required for developing and launching an app. PaaS is a complete development and deployment environment in the cloud, which provides tools and resources to develop and deliver everything from simple cloud-based apps to sophisticated, cloud-enabled enterprise applications. Like the Infrastructure as a service (IaaS), PaaS also requires infrastructure like servers and networking but works like a middleware between the Infrastructure and the user. It's an abstraction that makes it easy for the user to develop and deliver any app, without the need for any understanding about the infrastructure. PaaS is designed to support the complete web application lifecycle: building, testing, deploying, managing and updating. PaaS also makes the user free from buying and managing software licenses, application infrastructure and middleware, like Kubernetes or the development tools and other resources. It also allows the user to develop and manage the applications/services, and everything else is managed by the PaaS provider. Cloud Foundry is a kind of PaaS that can help to develop applications/services easily with convenience. Cloud Foundry is an open source, multi-cloud application platform as a service (PaaS) governed by the Cloud Foundry Foundation. The software was originally developed by VMware but later acquired by Pivotal Software (a joint venture company by EMC, VMware and General Electric) but in 2019 it was again transferred to VMware after the takeover of Pivotal by VMware.

The popularity of Cloud Foundry comes from its continuous delivery because it can support the complete application development lifecycle (starting from initial development to the final testing and deployment stages). The container-based architecture of Cloud Foundry can run apps in any programming language over a variety of cloud service providers. Because of its multi-cloud environment, a desirable cloud platform can be chosen by the developers to suit specific application workloads and can move such workloads as required (within a short time), without causing any changes to the application.

In Cloud Foundry, the deployed applications can access the external resources via an Open Service Broker API, which was launched in December 2016. In a platform, all external dependencies such as databases, messaging systems, file systems and so on are considered services. It allows administrators to create a marketplace of applications/services, from which users can use them on demand. Cloud Foundry supports various programming languages like Java, .NET, Ruby, Python, PHP and Go. In Cloud Foundry, the Docker lifecycle can be used to deploy Docker images that contain packed applications. The Cloud Foundry Application Runtime can also be deployed to various infrastructure providers like VMware's vSphere, OpenStack, Amazon Web Services, Microsoft Azure, IBM Cloud, Google Cloud Platform and Alibaba Cloud. However, some others can use the runtime using the Cloud Provider Interface (CPI) capability of the Cloud Foundry BOSH project. The Cloud Foundry platform can be used as an open-source software from the Cloud Foundry foundation or like a software product delivered as a service from various commercial providers and it's available to anyone as an open-source software. The "Cloud Foundry PaaS Certification program" from the Cloud Foundry Foundation, started in December 2015, and it certifies a Cloud Foundry Certified Provider.

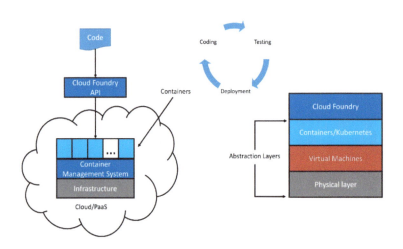

Cloud Foundry Layers

Usually in any PaaS, the physical layer stays at the bottom and above it are the Virtual Machines and Containers/Kubernetes. The topmost layer is always for the server but in case of Cloud Foundry, it's server less and Cloud Foundry stays on top of all these layers. This makes it a perfect abstraction for the users to develop and deliver applications/services without the need to know about the infrastructure. Any application/service can be developed using the Cloud Foundry API and can be deployed and tested in the containers. Such containers are self-maintained by Cloud Foundry's container management systems like Diego/Gardean. In this way users can easily develop and deliver applications/services to the customers without much complexity.

Features of Cloud Foundry

- Application execution, portability, auto-scaling and deployment.

- Application lifecycle and health management.

- Centralized platform administration and logging.

- Provides dynamic routing and external logging of components.

- Maintains infrastructure security and cloud provider integration.

- Integration with development tools and support for various IaaS providers.

Pros and cons

Pros	Cons
<ul><li>Easy development, testing and deployment of applications/services using the Cloud Foundry's API.</li><li>Supports various programming languages like Java, .NET, Ruby, Python, PHP and Go.</li></ul>	<ul><li>Cloud Foundry does not support stateful containers.</li><li>It has logging issues and even though the platform supports showing logs, it doesn't appear to persist these logs anywhere.</li><li>Despite claiming to be always a universal solution</li></ul>

• Users can develop applications/servic es without the need to configure/manage the infrastructure and Cloud Foundry is an abstraction that eliminates the need to know anything about the infrastructure. • Supports memory and disk space limit allocation for individual applications.	and supporting various programming languages and frameworks, Cloud Foundry is best suited for applications that are built in accordance with the Twelve-Factor App methodology.

Unlike any other PaaS, Cloud Foundry provides the best solutions and development tools to the user for developing any application/service easily. As this PaaS maintains a high level of abstraction, users don't have to deal much with the underlying infrastructure and can develop applications/services in various programming languages. Therefore, Cloud Foundry can be considered to be the best open-source PaaS for the development and delivery of any application/service conveniently.

Disaster management using FOSS tools

Data can be vital and it needs storage, but data can be lost as a result of any disaster that can occur from any physical damage to the storage hardware or from any software bug or virus, and that's why data should be stored using a suitable backup method and on a reliable storage. However, backup can be automated and can be done regularly using a powerful backup tool.

Types of backup

There are various types of backup but the most commonly used backup types are – full backup, differential backup, incremental backup and reverse incremental backup. Most of these backups can be done manually or can be automated using a backup software and the backup is kept in the repository. A repository is a place where data is kept safely on storage media in an organized manner.

- **Full backup:** In this type of backup, all the stored data is copied from the source storage (usually hard drive) to a storage media and kept in the repository. In this method, every time the backup of all the stored data is copied to the storage media and kept in the repository.

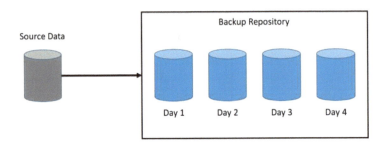

Full Backup

For example, if on day-1 the full backup is done for all the stored data then on day-2 also all the stored/changed data will be copied to the backup storage media and kept in the repository. Same thing will be done for day-3, day-4 and so on. That's why for doing regular full backups, the size of the storage media should be the same or more than the source storage. This type of backup is reliable but needs a lot of storage space on a regular basis. This type of backup takes a lot of time to backup but can be restored quickly and easily.

- **Differential backup:** A differential backup is done by comparing the differences in data between the first full backup and the changed source data. At first, a full backup is created and then differential backups are created subsequently, and only the changed data since the last full backup are only copied to the storage media. In this way every time the data gets changed on the source storage, a differential backup for only the changed data is created and stored in the repository.

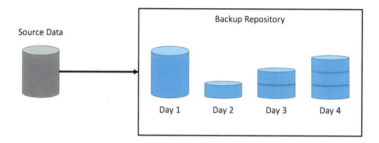

Differential Backup

For example, on day-1 a full backup is created for the source data and then if there is any change on the source data (compared to the last full backup) then another backup for the changed data is created on day-2. In the same way, if any change occurs again then the same thing will be done on day-3, day-4 and so on. This type of backup is faster than a full backup and initially takes less storage space but the backup file may grow bigger in size, after a certain number of backups. That's why this type of backup is usually done on a HDD or a tape.

- **Incremental backup:** This backup is done by creating a full backup first and then subsequent backups are created for the last changed data and it is done by comparing the source data and the last backup data. This type of backup differs from differential backup in a way that incremental backup only copies the data which was changed since last backup but differential backup copies data which was changed since the last full backup.

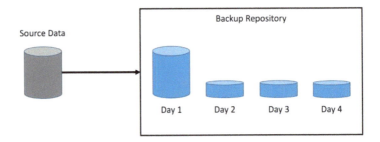

Incremental Backup

For example on day-1 a full backup is created and then if any change happens to the source data, then a backup is done on day-2 but only the changed data is copied to the backup storage media. In the same way if any change happens to the source data again, then only the changed data – when compared to the backup data of day-2, are only copied as backup data on day-3 and the same thing is done for day-4 again. Incremental backup is better than differential backup because it takes less storage space and time to backup data. That's why this type of backup can also be done on optical discs like DVDs and Blu-ray.

- **Reverse-incremental backup:** Reverse-incremental backup is almost similar to an incremental backup but in this backup the incremental backups are also injected to the full backup to create a synthetic full backup. At first a full backup is created and then the changed source data is copied as an incremental backup on a storage media but it is also injected to the full backup. Then again if any change happens to source data – subsequent incremental backups are created on storage media and

also incremental backups are injected to the full backup
– creating a synthetic full backup.

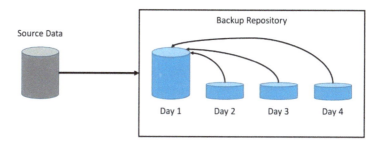

Reverse Incremental Backup

For example, on day-1 a full backup is created for the
source data and if any change happens to the source
data then an incremental backup is created on day-2 for
only the changed data, but the incremental backup is
also injected to the full backup that was created on day-
1. In the same way incremental and synthetic backups
are created for day-3, day-4 and so on. This backup
process takes little longer than a normal incremental
backup, but takes very less time to restore the backup –
as the synthetic full backup can be used for restoration
easily. This type of backup can also be done on optical
disc but tapes are usually suitable for creating the
synthetic full backup.

Among all these types of backups – incremental and reverse-
incremental backup are often preferred. Such kind of backup
can also be done for home and personal use, but it also needs
backup software to accomplish that and many backup software
uses a method called Continuous Data Protection (CDP), and

with CDP the source data is automatically copied to the backup storage media continuously in real-time, whenever there is any change to the source data.

Storage types

Backup can be done on various storage media like hard drive, optical disc (CD/DVD) and tapes (digital audio tape). Hard drive is the most common storage media used for backup but choosing the right hard drive and capacity is the biggest challenge. Usually there are two types of hard drives, one is called Hard Disk Drive (HDD) and another is Solid State Drive (SSD). HDDs are traditional old type hard drives, whereas SSDs are the latest ones and are much faster than the HDDs. HDDs use a magnetic disk to store data and have mechanical parts, whereas SSDs use only microchips called NAND flash to store data and have no mechanical parts. That's why SSDs are more durable when compared to HDDs and are less prone to data loss from physical impact/shock. However, SSDs are way too expensive when compared to HDDs and are not usually preferred for storing huge amounts of data.

Hard drives: HDD (left) and SSD (right)

While selecting an HDD one should look for the RPM of the drive and drives with 7200RPM are better. The transfer rate of HDDs depends on its RPM and a SATA-III 7,200 RPM HDD can achieve a transfer rate up to 300 MB/s, where an SSD can reach up to 600MB/s. SSDs are faster than normal HDDs but they can't hold data for a longer period when compared to HDDs. A typical SSD can hold data up to 10 yrs. without power but an HDD can hold data up to 30yrs or more. As SDDs use electrical charge to store data and because of internal electrical leakage, sometimes data gets corrupted sooner than HDDs, whereas HDDs use magnetic disk to store data electro-magnetically. Choosing the capacity (GB) of the hard drive is also a very important thing, because a hard drive with very less capacity will create problems in the future and a hard drive with much higher capacity could also waste money, if all of it's storage space is not used. Therefore, a proper plan should be made before choosing the right capacity of the backup drive.

Apart from the hard drive, backup can also be done using an optical disc. An optical disc is a kind of storage media, on which data can be written or read using a laser beam. There are various types of optical disc like Compact Disc (CD), Digital Versatile Disc (DVD) and Blu-ray DVD. A CD can store data up to 700 MB, DVD can store 4.7 GB (single-sided, single-layer)/8.5 GB (single-sided, double-layer)/9.4 GB (double-sided, single-layer)/17.08 GB (double-sided, double-layered) and a Blu-ray has the capacity of 25 GB (single-layer)/50GB (double-layer).

<u>Optical disc</u>

Creating backups on optical discs is also preferred because it's a cheaper option – as the price of an optical disc is reasonable and data can also be stored on them safely. But there are two formats of optical disc – Recordable (R) and Rewritable (RW)/Recordable Erasable (RE) Recordable disc can be used only once for backup, whereas a rewritable disc can be used many times to backup data. Therefore, DVD rewritable (DVD-RW/+RW) and Blu-ray Recordable Erasable (BD-RE) are preferred for doing regular backups. Moreover, the lifespan of an optical disc is more than 100yrs and that's why creating backups on optical discs will be more reliable than a hard drive.

Optical discs are a better option for creating backups but any optical disc can suffer from physical damage if not handled carefully. Any scratch or cosmetic damage on the readable surface of the optical disc can corrupt its stored data. That's why another better option is to backup data on tapes. Tapes used to backup digital data are called Linear Tape-Open (LTO) Ultrium and a LTO-8 tape cartridge can store up to 12 TB of uncompressed data and 30 TB of compressed data.

LTO tape cartridge

Tapes are good for making multiple copies of a backup because tapes are good for duplication and replication. It also takes very less time to restore a backup using tapes and that's why many data centers still use tape drives in their backup repository. However, using tapes for backup at home won't be reasonable because the tape cartridges cost more than any optical disc, but LTO Ultrium tapes have better shelf-life when compared to SDDs and can retain data up to 30yrs.

Besides these storage media, backup can also be done on any online cloud storage drive like the google drive. But for doing backup of large quantities of data to any cloud storage, a high speed internet is required, and the internet bandwidth should be good and stable. It's also not a good idea to store large files on cloud storage drives, because during any network problem it will be difficult to restore the backup data and cloud storage providers are also not always reliable.

Popular FOSS Tools for backup

Backup can be done reliably on a reliable storage using a good backup software and there are various Free Open Source Software (FOSS) tools available for backup. However, choosing the right tool can carry on the backup process conveniently. The following FOSS tools can be used to maintain the backup of data and can be restored easily.

- **Bacula:** This is a popular FOSS enterprise-level computer backup tool for heterogeneous networks and can automate any backup that needs intervention from a systems administrator or computer operator. It supports various Operating Systems including Linux, UNIX, Windows, and macOS and a range of professional backup devices including tape libraries. Bacula can be configured and used with a command line console, GUI or web interface and the back-end, which is a catalog of information, stored by MySQL, PostgreSQL, or SQLite. It was developed in January 2000 by Kern Sibbald. It was written in C and C++, and both are very powerful computer languages. Bacula is open-source and released under the AGPL version 3 license but there is an exception to permit the linking with OpenSSL and distributing the Windows binaries. The firewall administration and network security of Bacula is easy to use because the TCP/IP client–server communication uses standard ports and services instead of RPC for NFS, SMB, etc. It uses the CRAM-MD5 configurable client–server authentication and the GZIP/LZO client-side compression, which reduces the network bandwidth consumption and it runs separately from hardware compression done by any backup device. Apart from that Bacula also uses Transport Layer Security (TLS) network communication encryption, MD5/SHA file integrity verification, Cyclic Redundancy Check (CRC) data block integrity verification, Public Key Infrastructure (PKI) backup data encryption, Network Data Management Protocol (NDMP) enterprise version plugin and supports cloud backup with some Amazon S3 or Amazon Simple Storage Service file storage services.

- **Amanda:** This is another FOSS backup tool that can backup data from multiple computers of a network. It uses a client-server architecture and the server connects with the client to backup data at a scheduled time. It was developed at the University of Maryland of USA and was written in C and Perl language. The commercial version called the Amanda Enterprise Edition was developed by Zmanda Inc. It can run on almost any Unix Operating System and also on Linux, Windows, Mac OS X and Solaris. Amanda can backup data on both tape and disk drives. The two exceptional features of Amanda is that it supports tape-spanning and if the backup doesn't fit in one tape then it can be saved on multiple tapes by splitting that data. Another special feature is the intelligent scheduler, which can optimize the use of computing resources across many backup runs.

- **Back in Time:** This backup FOSS tool is exclusively written for the Linux Operating System only. It was developed by a group of people, namely Oprea Dan, Bart de Koning, Richard Bailey, Germar Reitze and Taylor Raack in 2008 and was written in Python. This backup tool is distributed along with many Linux distributions. Back in Time is a reliable backup tool similar to Apple's Time Machine. This tool uses Rsync (utility used for synchronizing files between various storage) as a backend and uses hard links for file storage and that eliminates unnecessary usage of disk space, when there are identical snapshots of a file at different times and remains unchanged. This hard link method also makes it easy to look at the snapshots of the system at different times and can help in the removal of any unnecessary snapshot. Back in Time also supports encryption of backups and backup over SSH.

Disaster can happen at any time, and keeping the data safe is the biggest challenge. There are various backup methods available and backup can be done on various storage types, but choosing the right backup method and storage, can help keep the data safe and secured. Such backups can be automated using a reliable backup tool and choosing the right tool can make the backup/restore process much easier. That's why one can take advantage of any FOSS backup tool to keep data safe.

Top 10 business apps for Android Enterprise

Business processes can be automated and improved using a sophisticated IT infrastructure, but for that we need state of the art operating system and apps. One such operating system that one must have for running a substantial business is Android Enterprise and the top 10 apps that are discussed below. Android Enterprise provides Enterprise Mobility Management (EMM) technology that is required for processing the business data of the enterprise safely. The EMM tools and processes can be used for a business process to manage and secure the connected mobile devices and mobile computing solutions. It's also used to manage the Bring Your Own Device (BYOD) policy and prevent any unauthorized access. BYOD is the policy used by many enterprises to allow their users to use their personal mobile devices to access their private network and data.

Three main technologies of EMM

EMM is used by Android Enterprise to secure and manage the enterprise data using various tools and the API. It uses the following technologies to make any mobile device access the database of any enterprise safely:

- **Mobile Device Management (MDM):** It enables IT administrators to apply security policies on mobile devices used within their network and it gives life-cycle management functions like locking, data wiping and controlling the mobile devices.

- **Mobile App Management (MAM):** This also gives security administration and life-cycle management functions but it applies to the applications running on the mobile devices. With the help of MAM administrators can manage and distribute apps among the mobile devices connected to the network.

- **Mobile Identity Management (MIM):** With this technology the administrators can secure system access, and MIM ensures that only authorized users and devices can access any protected data. It can compile various types of identity management including Digital Certifications, Single Sign-On, Device Enrollment and Authentication.

Together these technologies of EMM provides the tools necessary to protect any corporate data and prevents any kind of system breach. It also helps to manage and control mobile devices remotely, including the OS and the apps installed. In that way employees can use their personal mobile devices using the BYOD policy and can also work from home during any crisis. EMM also provides the ability to lock any mobile device remotely and can be used if any devices get stolen or lost. With EMM, the IT administrator can even wipe off all the sensitive data from any mobile device whenever required, which can be done if the device is lost or hacked. EMM also has the ability to track down any mobile device and can be located, when it's lost. EMM gives data separation feature, enabling only authorized apps and users to access the permitted data, and keeps the personal data/apps of the user separately from the system.

Components of Android Enterprise

The EMM is integrated with Android Enterprise using three components: *EMM console*, *Android Device Policy*, and *Managed Google Play*. The EMM console is the web interface that can be used by the administrator for managing apps and applying policies to the mobile devices. Android Device Policy is an app that must be installed in the mobile device so that the EMM policies are enabled in that device. Managed Google Play is a customized version of the Google Play store that provides only permitted apps to the connected mobile devices.

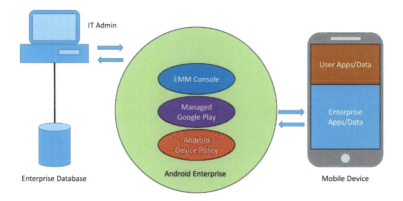

Components of Android Enterprise

Top 10 android enterprise/business apps

In order to make a business process safe and secure, one must use a reliable business app and can manage it conveniently with the tap of a finger. As there are many apps available in the app store, it's often very difficult to find the right app for your business. However, Capterra Inc. is one company that helps in finding the right app for your business. The company assists consumers with selecting the right app for their needs. It also reviews all kinds of apps, and rates them according to their performance and features. The following top 10 list of apps may be helpful for your business and are listed as per the reviews and ratings done by Capterra.

1. **NetSuite:** This app is offered by Oracle America, Inc and is one of the best enterprise android apps. It enables unparalleled access to the #1 Cloud Business Software Suite, which is the unified business management suite, encompassing ERP / financials, CRM and ecommerce. NetSuit helps in maintaining your business as you do from your PC, and with mobile-only features and out-of-the-box support for 19 languages, this app is useful for almost all types of people and business.

The main features of this app are:

- Get instant business snapshots, with full dashboard support.

- Check KPIs from anywhere.

- Manage Time and Expenses.

- Log Inbound and Outbound Phone Calls.

- Approve records and trigger key business actions.

- Tap approve expense reports and purchase orders.

- Plan workdays with full NetSuite calendar access.

- Harness the power of Saved Searches.

- Quickly Create, View and Edit records.

- Search and view lists of records.

- Create Favorites for convenient lookup of record lists.

2. **HoneyBook:** This app is offered by HoneyBook Inc and it's another enterprise app that helps maintain your business efficiently. It helps in getting the right client and can reply to questions quickly, send professional invoices, contracts, quotes and brochures. This app can manage your clients and helps grow your business quickly. HoneyBook can let your business run seamlessly and stay organized from anywhere. You'll be able to access client details, get notifications & respond, send invoices & use templates from anywhere from your mobile device.

The main features of this app are:

- Manage your client dashboard from anywhere and manage the client data in one place.

- Send messages and files to the clients using personalized templates including invoice, contracts, emails, brochures and questionnaires.

- Send mobile friendly invoices to the clients and get your payment faster. Payments are safe and secure with 24/7 fraud monitoring.

- Get instant notifications about client's inquiries, messages and payments. You Can check your availability and schedule without leaving the app and also review, add and check off tasks wherever you are.

3. **Dynamics 365:** This app is offered by Microsoft Corporation and is one enterprise app which is an essential business solution for busy professionals who need to engage with customers while staying productive at work and on the go. With this app one can arrive prepared for every appointment and update notes, tasks, and attachments – along with relevant service and sales records – while the details are still fresh. It provides salespeople, agents, and supervisors with the best tools for managing and updating their data, either online or offline. Dynamics 365 Can be deployed on any android device seamlessly with minimum configuration.

The main features of this app are:

- New look and compact layout with stacked elements, optimized to give essential info at a glance.

- The workspace and personalized action hub gives you the provision to do common tasks quickly.

- Has enhanced note taking experience and seamless access to camera and other device capabilities.

- Can give offline access with synchronization, so that you can work on the go.

- Access your activities, accounts, contacts, and leads from an easy-to-use home page.

- Has guided contextual business processes.

- Helps track progress for key performance indicators visually with charts.

- Access your personalized views of lists and grids so that you see the data most important to you.

4. **Genbook:** This app is offered by Genbook Inc and with this app one can instantly book appointments with favorite businesses, conveniently. Get connected with various local service professionals and book or pay, right from your Android phone. Genbook lets you deal with your appointments, on the go and can choose the time that's right for you, at your convenience, 24/7.

   The main features of this app are:

   - Book from the favorites list at any time.

   - Easy viewing of the updated business details, services, and prices.

   - Get real-time availability and instant confirmation.

   - Booking history and upcoming appointments can be managed.

   - Reschedule, rebook or cancel with convenience.

   - Nearby businesses can be discovered and booked easily.

   - Verified Customer Reviews & Ratings can be viewed.

5. **Zoho One:** This app is offered by Zoho CorporationBusiness and it has a suite of apps that helps manage your business on

your mobile device. It has all the comprehensive apps for your business and has centralized administrative control from one single console. Zoho One has a suite of apps that lets you gain control of every business needs like recruitment, launching your website, marketing your product, catering to customers and so on. All permissions across the business data, such as user management, email hosting, mail management and security policies can be accessed by the administrators and owners of the Zoho One organization, and the Zoho One app is now also available to all the Zoho one users of your organization.

The main features of this app are:

- Admin privileges like add a user, assign apps, roles, formulate security policies, create groups, etc, from your mobile device.

- Get real-time notifications for reset password, assign apps etc, from the users in your organization immediately.

- Personalization options like create a customized email address to all your employees and personalize their accounts.

- Launch all your apps within the suite with just a single tap and can request access to the apps you need from the admin and also discover apps that can be installed.

- Search all your data across Zoho apps without any hassle and work with other Zoho apps too. Find all the needed information and narrow down your search results with fine filters to find relevant information without switching between apps.

6. **17hats:** This app is offered by 17hats and can help maintain any small scale business. It can guide through organizing, managing and growing the business using a mobile device. 17hats lets you keep you in touch with your business while you are on the go.

The main features of this app are:

- The dashboard lets you check recent client activity, pending documents and upcoming tasks.

- Quickly respond to any business email using various email templates.

- Create and edit contacts and projects and also, quickly access details like email addresses, phone numbers and locations to name a few.

- Easily view the calendar and adjust it on the go.

- Documents can be quickly sent and countersign a contract or view a completed questionnaire.

- Workflows can be easily assigned to leads and clients.

7. **Odoo:** This app is offered by Odoo S.A. and it's a suite of open source business apps that covers all the business needs like CRM, eCommerce, Accounting, Inventory, Point of Sale, Project Management, and more. The mobile app offers a smooth and friendly user experience that has been carefully built to ensure quick and seamless user adoption. It has the fluidity and full integration that cover the needs of even the most complex companies. Odoo gives the flexibility to add apps whenever a new need is determined according to the growth of your company, adding one app at a time as the business evolves and customer base grows.

The main features of this app are:

- Configure the pricelist at the backend.

- Tracking products of the customers.

- Manage and publish banners separately.
- Product sliders and sliders modes.

- Configure the selection of products, either automatic or manual.

- Manage push notifications.

- Configure action to trigger on customer's product/category/custom collection page.

- Manage unlimited featured product categories using the app builder.

- Homepage with highlights of the popular categories.

8. **vCita:** This app is offered by vCita and it helps in managing your day-to-day activities like a pro, and lets you build a business that you need. Do appointment scheduling, billing & invoicing, client management and even marketing! Simply sign up, log in and stay connected to your business and your clients 24/7. vCita lets you provide a seamless customer experience, allowing leads and clients to book appointments, pay for services, correspond with your business and share documents via your website, Facebook page or directly from Google search.

   The main features of this app are:

   - View Calendar, do scheduling, client management, payments and marketing.

   - Get more bookings from your website, Facebook page or through Google.

   - Send friendly automated meeting reminders to reduce no-shows.

   - Actionable invoices and payment reminders prevents any unpleasant collection calls.
   - Client records with detailed client cards helps create relationships.

   - Engage with clients and offer last-minute deals with coupons and campaigns.

9. **mHelpDesk:** This app is offered by mHelpdesk and it saves time and lets you stay productive even when you're not in the office. It gives you the ability to manage schedules, view job progress, check in on field technicians, send estimates and invoices, and much more. It also can make communication between office and field staff a breeze with real-time updates, and can quickly create estimates from templates on your mobile device on the fly. Then email or print them for your customer immediately to get ahead of the competition. mHelpDesk payments helps you get paid faster, easier and on the go and also integrates with other payment options (PayPal, Stripe and Authorize.NET). This app also works offline and syncs with the database whenever online.

The main features of this app are:

- Work online or offline and with the offline feature, your team can continue to work even when a Wi-Fi or cell signal isn't available and the app automatically syncs as soon as a connection is found.

- Simplified scheduling lets you check your own schedule or your team's schedule, and create new jobs and appointments directly within the app. mHelpDesk can schedule with Google Calendar for extra efficiency.

- Professional estimates, on site lets you create and send estimates on the go, using professional templates that you've selected and customized. When the work is done, you can turn the estimate into an invoice with a few button clicks.

- Get invoices paid faster by emailing professional-looking invoices directly from your phone, allowing you to take payment immediately.

- Customer support can be done easily by keeping all of your lead, customer, and job details within the app, your team always has the information they need. And with automated email and SMS (text) alerts, team members and customers can always have the latest information on job status.

- Field and office are connected easily and communication between office and field techs is seamless. Data is updated automatically so that everyone is on the same page, and the app saves you time and energy in connecting field and office staff so that everyone can focus on job quality and customer service

10. **Karbon:** This app is offered by KarbonHQ and it provides a truly collaborative platform for accounting firms to manage workflows, communicate with teams and deliver exceptional client work — from anywhere. It's embedded in your workflow, so your team can estimate work and track time right where the work happens. It lets you confidently scope work, automate data collection, scale client onboarding, anticipate bottlenecks and automate recurring work for the future. The communication is in one place so you know your team has everything they need to get started and see where every job stands to ensure accountability across teams. Karbon can analyze team performance, improve inefficient processes, identify your quality clients and inform future planning to improve profitability.

The main features of this app are:

- Discuss about the work with your team directly on the emails, notes and tasks at hand.

- Helps transform emails into personal tasks or delegate to your team.

- Assign notes, tasks, email and work to colleagues.

- Swipe and clear items that are not required.

- Identify what's important using a Low-Priority filter.

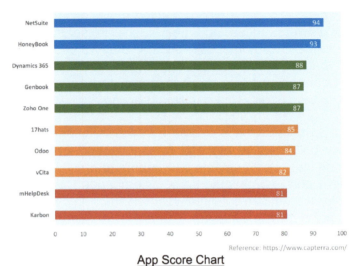

Reference: https://www.capterra.com/

App Score Chart

Among the above top 10 apps – NetSuite, HoneyBook and Dynamics 365 seems to be the best apps as per the performance and feature is concerned, but you can use any app from the list as per your business need. The above android apps rated by Capterra can be considered to be the perfect apps for the business use, but any other android app may also suit your business requirement. Therefore, choosing the right app for your business could require your own intervention and knowledge.

Python is best for Machine Learning

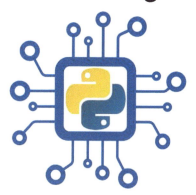

Machine Learning (ML) is a technology used with the help of algorithms, to make any software process improve through experience. ML is a part of Artificial Intelligence (AI) and it uses training data to improve the decisions and predictions, without the need of any explicit programming. In the business world, ML is used to resolve business problems and is also referred to as predictive analysis. To run any static process, it's possible to program a computer using specific algorithms, but when it comes to dynamic processes, it must modify its program and improve the algorithm to handle any such process in real-time. ML was first conceived by Arthur Samuel of IBM in 1952 and he created the world's first ML program to run checkers video games on IBM 701 computers. There are mainly two objectives of ML, one is to classify data models, which have been developed using I/O data, and the other one is to predict future outputs based on that data. These two objectives can be achieved using various learning algorithms, and also with the help of a powerful programming language like Python.

Types of learning approaches

In ML an agent can be made intelligent using various learning approaches and algorithms. In such a learning process, the ML has to go through three stages – training, validation and testing.

This is done in order to process the input data and modify the algorithm for improving prediction and performance. There are various types of learning approaches available but the three main traditionally used learning approaches include Supervised, Unsupervised and Reinforcement learning.

Supervised learning: As the name suggests, this learning approach involves training the agent by a supervisor, which is usually the user. Here, the training is given to the agent using a set of training data, as examples or data models. The data contains a label and a feature. The set of data also contains the mapping of the input and output data based on the data model. So, when any new data is fed into the agent as input data, it also generates new output data based on the data model. A simple example of a data model would be a table containing rows and columns, which has data about various laptops with different specifications and price tags. So, by looking at the table one can understand which laptops are expensive and which are cheap. If this model is used for ML training then the agent would be able to predict if a laptop with higher CPU speed will cost more or less. The accuracy and method of processing the data depends on the algorithm and the training data used for the ML. If the output data is not satisfactory, then again modification to the algorithm and the training data is done by the supervisor. Then again, the agent is fed with new data and output is gathered (as a feedback to the supervisor). In case the output is not satisfactory then more modifications are done, and the cycle continues until the agent is stable and matured. Here, the Naive Bayes algorithm is used because it's best known for its ability to classify and predict data.

Naive Bayes algorithm works on the following formula:

$$P(A|B) = \frac{P(B|A)\, P(A)}{P(B)}$$

Where,

A, B = Events
P(A|B) = probability of A given B is true
P(B|A) = probability of B given A is true
P(A), P(B) = the independent probabilities of A and B

However, if you need to understand the above formula in simple English, then it will be as follows:

$$Posterior = \frac{Prior \times Likelihood}{Evidence}$$

Now, the *Posterior* probability for supervised training would be the expected prediction data. To get that data, the *Prior* probability data is always updated. You can say that it's like a history data and the *Likelihood* is the data that you can assume from previous events but *Evidence* is the data that is already known and correct.

Example:
If the chances of getting attacked by a dangerous computer virus is 1% but the detection of any virus by a cyber-security software is 10%, and 90% of viruses are not harmful, then the probability of getting any harm from a dangerous virus would be:

$$P(Virus) = \frac{P(Harm) \times P(Harm)}{P(Virus)}$$

$$= \frac{1\% \times 90\%}{10\%} = 9\%$$

Algorithm:
1. Separate the training data by class.
2. Summarize datasets by finding the mean and standard deviation using the formulas:
   Mean $= \frac{\Sigma |x-\mu|}{N}$, x is the feature data and N is the number of feature data. $\mu = (x_1 + x_2 + x_3... + x_n)/N$.

Standard deviation = $\sqrt{\frac{1}{N}\sum_{i=1}^{N}}$ $(x_i - \mu)^2$, x_i is the featured data starting with the index value of i.

3. Summarize data by class.
4. Calculate the probability using Gaussian Probability Density Function formula:

$\frac{1}{\partial\sqrt{2\pi}}$ $e^{-\frac{1}{2}(\frac{x-\mu}{\partial})^2}$, μ is the mean and ∂ is the standard deviation.

5. Predict class probability using the Naive Bayes classifier.

Unsupervised learning: This learning approach requires no supervisor and the agent uses unlabeled data for input processing. The algorithm used in this learning approach helps the agent to find structure in its input, so that it can group or cluster data based on its patterns. Here, the input data is clustered by the agent accordingly and can also discover hidden data. After clustering the data, the agent tries to find similarities between them and creates a relationship model. This learning requires a proper learning environment and better the input data, better will be the learning. The algorithm used in this learning is called K-Means and the formula is:

$$J = \sum_{j=1}^{k} \sum_{i=1}^{n} \| x_i^{(j)} - c_j \|^2$$

Where,
J = objective function
k = number of clusters
n = number of cases
$x_i^{(j)}$ = case i
c_j = centroid for cluster j
$x_i^{(j)} - c_j$ = distance function

Clustering can also be done using a simple Euclidean distance formula:

$$\sqrt{(x_x - x_1)^2 + (x_y - y_1)^2}$$

Where,

x_x & x_y are observed values and x_1 & y_1 are actual/centroid values.

Example:
You can divide the following dataset into two clusters:

Data ID	X	Y
1	1	2
2	3	4
3	5	6
4	7	8
5	9	10

First you find the centroids and create the two clusters (C1, C2) by taking the values of two Data ID (1,2):

Clusters	X	Y	Centroid
C1	1	2	(1,2)
C2	3	4	(3,4)

Now you find in which cluster (C1 or C2) the next values of Data ID (3) will be included by using the Euclidean distance formula as follows:

$C1 = \sqrt{(5-1)^2 + (6-2)^2}$
$\quad = \sqrt{(4)^2 + (4)^2}$
$\quad = \sqrt{32} = 5.65$
$C2 = \sqrt{(5-3)^2 + (6-4)^2}$
$\quad = \sqrt{(2)^2 + (2)^2}$
$\quad = \sqrt{8} = 2.28$

Now, as the value of C2 is less than C1, the Data ID (3) will be clustered with C2.

Next, the new centroid values of C2 will be:

$$C2 = ((X_{C2} + X_3)/2,(Y_{C2} + Y_3)/2)$$
$$= ((3+5)/2,(4+6)/2)$$
$$= 4,5$$

Similarly, the values for next Data IDs can be found by using the new centroids of C2 and carry on the clustering process.

Algorithm:
1. Cluster data into *k* groups, where *k* is predefined.
2. Select random cluster centroids from the k points.
3. Allocate data to the nearest clusters according to the Euclidean distance calculations.
4. Calculate new cluster centroids for next data.
5. Repeat steps from 2 to 4 until no further clustering is possible.

Reinforcement learning: This type of learning works based on reward/penalty policy, and the agent is programmed to do certain predefined functions to perform in an environment. After executing the functions, the agent gets feedback from the environment, either as a reward or penalty. This also changes the state of the environment and the agent also gathers the state of the environment as an input. Depending on the state and reward values, the agent takes decisions. Depending on the rewards and state changes, the agent improves its quality of performance. This type of learning approach is used in service robots to train them in certain environments and it doesn't require any training datasets or data models. Here, the Q-learning algorithm is used and works with the following formula:

$$Q_{new}(s_t, a_t) \leftarrow Q_{old}(s_t, a_t) + \; . \; (r_t + \gamma \; . \; max_a Q(s_{t+1}, a) - Q_{old}(s_t, a_t))$$

Where,
Q_{new} is the new state of the agent
s_t is the state of the agent in time *t*
a_t is the action taken by the agent in time $t.\alpha$
α is the learning rate
r_t is the reward in time *t*

γ is the discount factor

Example:
If the agent takes actions (A_1, A_2, A_3, A_4) and causes state changes (S_1, S_2, S_3, S_4) and receives a set of rewards R, then the Q values will be initialized and rewards data will be created as follows:

Q =

State S	A_1	A_2	A_3	A_4
S_1	0	0	0	0
S_2	0	0	0	0
S_3	0	0	0	0
S_4	0	0	0	0

R =

State S	A_1	A_2	A_3	A_4
S_1	0		0	1
S_2	0	0		0
S_3		0	0	1
S_4	0		0	1

Here, the reward values are either 1 or 0 based on the actions.

If the agent is in state S_4, then there are 3 possible actions that can change the state to S_1, S_3, and S_4. This will be calculated using a simplified formula:

Q(sate, action) = R(state, action) + γ × Max[Q(next state, all actions)]

Q(S_1, A_4) = R(S_1, A_4) + 0.8 × Max[Q(S_4, A_1),(S_4, A_3),(S_4, A_4)]
       = 1 + 0.8 × 0 = 1

Here, the value of Max[Q(next state, all actions)] is zero because the Q values were initialized to zero.

So, as the new Q values for Q(S$_1$, A$_4$) is 1, the Q values will be updated:

Q =

State S	A$_1$	A$_2$	A$_3$	A$_4$
S$_1$	0	0	0	1
S$_2$	0	0	0	0
S$_3$	0	0	0	0
S$_4$	0	0	0	0

Similarly, the next states will be determined by the agent and the Q values will keep on updating.

Algorithm:
1. Agent starts in state (s$_t$) and Q values are initialized.
2. Take action a$_t$ and wait for a reward (r$_t$) and state (s$_t$) change.
3. Update the reward (r$_t$) and state (s$_t$) values.
4. Calculate the next action using the Q-learning formula
5. Update Q values.

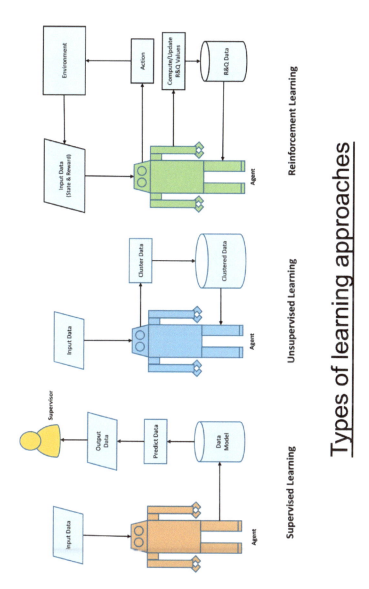

Types of learning approaches

Among the three learning approaches – Supervised learning is used only when both the input and output data is available along with the data model. Unsupervised learning is used only when the input data is available and Reinforcement learning is required when there is no training data and the agent is required to be trained from the working environment. Apart from these, there are many other learning approaches like Self learning,

99

Feature learning, Sparse dictionary learning, Anomaly detection, Robot learning and Association rule learning.

Hardware & Software for ML

To run any computer program (algorithm) a Central Processing Unit (CPU) is required. Most of the CPU hardware contains multiple cores but such CPUs are designed for serial operations and don't provide high throughput. However, a Graphics Processing Unit (GPU) can have a higher number of cores compared to a CPU and has higher throughput also. A CPU has more cache memory that can be used for complex operations but a GPU can be used for simple operations even if it has lesser cache memory. That's why a GPU can be used for ML and with the help of Compute Unified Device Architecture (CUDA), it's possible to make GPUs work with ML, which is also known as General Purpose computing on Graphics Processing Units (GPGPU).

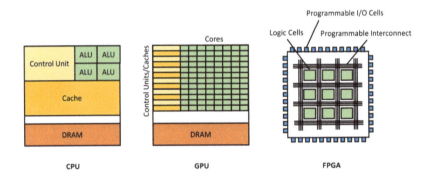

Different types of processors

Even though GPU is useful for ML, it has certain limitations and one such limitation is that its architecture cannot be customized for specific purposes. To overcome such limitations, a special kind of chip (hardware) is used and it's called Field

Programmable Gate Array (FPGA). Such a chip can be programmed as per the purpose and it's architecture can be customized for the specific agent in ML. An FPGA chip can contain thousands of memory units, which is greater than a GPU and can give better throughputs. Another advantage of using FPGA for ML is hardware acceleration, which can accelerate certain parts of an algorithm, making it more efficient than a GPU.

In order to take full advantage of the hardware, a good ML software can help build ML models as per requirement. There are many such software available online – either proprietary or free. Among the free ones, TensorFlow, Shogun, Apache Mahout, Pytorch, KNIME and Keras are more widely used and are the popular ones.

TensorFlow can help build ML solutions through its extensive interface of CUDA GPU. It provides support and functions for various applications of ML such as Computer Vision, NLP and Reinforcement Learning. This software is best suited for beginners in ML and is also used for education purposes too.

Shogun is a free software that supports languages like Python, R, Scala, C#, Ruby etc. It supports Vector Agents, Dimensionality Reduction, Clustering Algorithms, Hidden Markov Models and Linear Discriminant Analysis. Apache Mahout is a popular software that provides expressive Scala DSL and a distributed linear algebra framework for deep learning computations and native solvers for CPUs, GPUs as well as CUDA accelerators.

Pytorch was developed by Facebook's AI Research lab (FAIR) and it's mainly used for ML applications such as computer vision and natural language processing. It provides Tensor computing (like NumPy) with strong acceleration via graphics processing units (GPU) and supports deep neural networks built on a tape-based automatic differentiation system. The Tesla Autopilot (advanced driver-assistance system) used in Tesla cars of Tesla, Inc. was built using Pytorch.

KNIME – the Konstanz Information Miner, is a free software that can do data analysis/reporting using ML and data mining. It integrates various components for agent learning and data mining through its modular data pipelining "Lego of Analytics" concept. It provides a Graphical User Interface (GUI) and Java Database Connectivity (JDBC) features for blending various data sources for modelling, data analysis and visualization without, or with only minimal, programming. It has been used in areas like Pharmaceutical research, CRM customer data analysis, business intelligence, text mining and financial data analysis.

Keras provides a Python interface for artificial neural networks and it is well known for its modularity, speed, and ease of use. Keras supports backends like TensorFlow, Microsoft Cognitive Toolkit, Theano, and PlaidML. It's designed to enable fast experimentation with deep neural networks and it's designed to be user-friendly too.

Python for ML

Many types of programming languages like Python, C/C++, Java/JavaScript and R are used for ML but Python is most widely used because of its simplicity and features. It was created in the late 1980s, and first released in 1991, by Guido van Rossum as a successor to the ABC programming language.

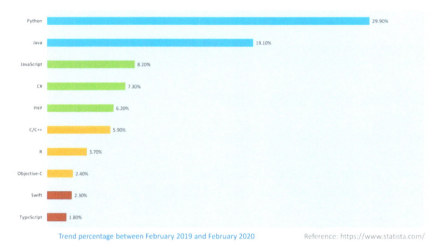

Trend percentage of programming languages

According to one survey done by Statista (a German company specializing in market and consumer data), Python is the most popular programming language in the world.

Unlike any other languages, Python gives the options to build ML programs using it's robust library and cross-compilation ability. Moreover, the syntax used in Python is more simple than C/C++ or Java.

For example, if a program is written to print the line "Hello World" using C/C++, Java and Python then it will be done as follows:

```cpp
// Print "Hello World" using C++ Program
#include <iostream>
int main() {
   std::cout << "Hello World!";
   return 0;
}
```

```java
// Print "Hello World" using Java
class HelloWorld {
```

```
    public static void main(String[] args) {
        System.out.println("Hello, World!");
    }
}
```

```python
# Print "Hello World" using Python
print('Hello, world!')
```

As you can see that to print the world "Hello World" using C/C++ and Java, many lines of code are needed, whereas in Python it can be done using a single line of code. The syntax used in Python is like an English language and it's easy to comprehend. Another special feature of Python when compared with other Object Oriented Programming (OOP) languages like C++ and Java is that it's possible to write Python code without making any use of the OOP concept. Python code can be used interpretively and any python statement can be interpreted using the interpreter prompt (>>>) and can be executed immediately without compiling the whole program, just like how interpreter works in BASIC programming language, but such a feature is not available in C/C++ or Java. In Python, variables are not required to be declared explicitly but in C/C++ and Java, the variables must be declared and their type remains static. For writing various types of code the ability of the programming language to handle various data types is also important and Python not only supports the primitive data types like Character, Boolean, Integer and Floating Point like C/C++,Java and R programming languages, but also additional data types like None, Complex Number, Dictionary and Tuple, which makes it more flexible to implement complex algorithms using Python code. Python also supports various mathematical functions with the help of its libraries, which makes it possible for programming different types of code for ML.

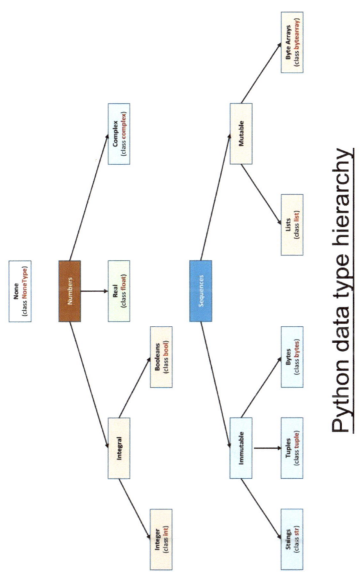

Python data type hierarchy

Cross-compilation is another great feature of Python and any code written in Python can be compiled to the C/C++ programming language. This can be done using CPython, which is a reference implementation of Python and can compile Python-like code to C/C++. Another reason for using Python for ML programming is the vast collection of libraries that are designed for ML and few such libraries include Numpy, Scipy,

Scikit-learn, Theano, TensorFlow, Keras, PyTorch, Pandas and Matplotlib. Such libraries make it possible to implement ML algorithms with greatest simplicity and convenience. The syntax used in Python is simple and any mathematical statements can be expressed with minimum coding work.

For example, if you need to implement the Naive Bayes algorithm using Python, then it can be done using the code:

```python
def bayes_algo(p_a, p_b_a, p_b_not_a):
    not_a = 1 - p_a
    p_b = p_b_a * p_a + p_b_not_a * not_a
    p_a_b = (p_b_a * p_a) / p_b
return p_a_b
```

You can see that it's very simple to implement such mathematical formula using the Python code, without the need to explicitly declare any variable or including any preprocessor/directive like #include, in C/C++.

As simple is better than complex, Python can be used for the development of various complex applications with optimized programming code. One empirical study found that Python is more productive than conventional languages, such as C/C++ and Java, for programming problems involving string manipulation or dictionary searches, and the memory consumption was also better than Java. That's why many large organizations like Google, Facebook, and Amazon, etc. use Python and it's also helping such companies to grow. Therefore, it can be concluded that Python is the best programming language for ML.

ABOUT THE AUTHOR

Debojit Acharjee has written many articles related to software technology and computer science. He has knowledge about various software technologies like Robot Process Automation (RPA), Artificial Intelligence (AI) & Machine Learning (ML), blockchain, DevOps, database management, and also knows many programming languages.